EAST-WEST RELATIONS:
IS DETENTE POSSIBLE?

Third in the third series of Rational Debate Seminars
sponsored by the American Enterprise Institute
held at
The Madison Hotel
Washington, D.C.

EAST-WEST RELATIONS: IS DETENTE POSSIBLE?

William E. Griffith
Walt W. Rostow

RATIONAL DEBATE SEMINARS

American Enterprise Institute
for Public Policy Research
Washington, D.C.

327.1
D87e
86725
Jan. 1974

Library of Congress Catalog Card Number 74-94772

FOREWORD

Professors Rostow and Griffith have brought the American Enterprise Institute's third season of Rational Debates to an impressive climax with their evaluation of the possibilities for East-West détente. We are now more than two decades into "the postwar period," and all of us are aware that powerful new forces are at work on both sides of the Iron Curtain. The principals in this debate had very much on their minds the invasion of Czechoslovakia and the Sino-Soviet eruptions on the Ussuri River, both events of special meaning for détente. Dr. Griffith and Dr. Rostow have spent many years in the search for a safe rapprochement with the Communist nations of the world. Their insights into the prospects for the future are, we believe, another important contribution to the dialogue on major public policy issues of our time.

November 3, 1969

WILLIAM J. BAROODY
President
American Enterprise Institute
for Public Policy Research

CONTENTS

FIRST LECTURE

WILLIAM E. GRIFFITH

When one tries to face up to such a vast and controversial subject as East-West relations, one may best begin with some definitions. First, détente, relaxation of tensions, is more than possible—it is here. International détente has often been interrupted but has basically continued since 1953—the death of Stalin and the Korean armistice. Partially reversed in 1958 by the second Berlin crisis, briefly displaced by the 1962 Cuban missile crisis—more recently, in spite of the Vietnam war, the invasion of Czechoslovakia, the permanent Middle Eastern crisis, and the current new escalatory cycle in the strategic arms race, détente has continued.

How does one assess its value? Détente may be considered valuable for its own sake, because it lessens the danger of nuclear or conventional war, lowers military expenditures, and thus provides more resources for peaceful, domestic needs, and transfers the great power conflict to the political and economic arena. From a different perspective, it may be considered valuable not only for all these reasons but also, indeed primarily, as a necessary precondition for the decisive transformation of major political problems in the interest of one or another major power: the reunification or the confirmation of the partition of Germany, Korea, or Vietnam; general or partial disarmament; or a Middle Eastern settlement.

Experience with détente since 1953 has shown that it tends to intensify the trend away from a bipolar toward a multipolar world. Détente makes the allies of each superpower fear war less. They therefore need be less united; they can more safely reassert their traditional nationalisms; and they are more tempted to try to maneuver one superpower against another (France or Rumania, for example). Conversely, during détente the superpowers have more opportunities for political and economic rivalry, through the unfreezing of the two power blocs and the resultant greater ability of each to exert its power in the other's sphere of influence.

The second necessary definition is of East-West relations: I understand them for the purposes of this paper to involve primarily the Soviet-United States superpower confrontation but also to include Western Europe and Japan on the one hand and the Chinese People's Republic and the East European states on the other. The underdeveloped, so-called "third" world is an object, not a subject of the competition of the two superpowers with each other and with China. Its own lack of power and unity makes its influence a result of, and dependent on, the East-West competition.

Within the Communist and the non-Communist worlds, détente has meant that alliances have loosened. Neither Moscow nor Washington now enjoys the degree of hegemony over its allies that it did before détente set in. More recently, the Soviet invasion of Czechoslovakia has slowed down the decline of NATO and further polarized Eastern Europe into pro- and anti-Soviet areas. The recent Sino-Soviet border clashes on the Ussuri River have dramatically revealed the fierce hostility which now dominates relations between Moscow and Peking. Moscow is probably beginning to regard Peking, as Peking is beginning to regard Moscow, as its main enemy, while their common enmity to the United States is moving toward second priority.

Let us now ask another question: what are the major new factors in international politics which affect détente? The first and most important is *the* major new factor in the post-1945 world: the existence of thermonuclear weapons and intercontinental missiles, plus the lack until now of any assured defense against these weapons, which have for the first time in history created a capability for destruction of all life on this globe. Thus the potential costs of war, given the danger that it will escalate to the thermonuclear level, have become much higher and its potential benefits much lower. There now exists, therefore, a powerful new incentive for all nations, particularly those with vast urban areas and highly developed economies, to try to lower the risk of a nuclear confrontation. Simultaneously, the enormous and at the moment greatly accelerating advantage of the two thermonuclear superpowers, the United States and the Soviet Union, over the other, smaller atomic powers, the United Kingdom, France, and China, has massively increased the relative power of the superpowers and lowered that of the others. Paradoxically, however, since the use of nuclear weapons is self-destructive, their power is not automatically translated into influence, as military power was before the atomic age. On the contrary, as the recent activities of North Korea demonstrate, smaller powers are now more easily able to defy their superpower opponent. Finally, the nature of atomic weapons makes the maintenance of alliances more difficult. The smaller alliance partners wish atomic aid from their superpower ally; but the two superpowers wish to prevent atomic proliferation in order, first, to lower the risk of nuclear war and, second, to maintain their unique superpower status. Thus American refusal to give atomic aid to France worsened relations between Paris and Washington; and Soviet reneging on its promise to give atomic aid to China was one of the major causes of the Sino-Soviet split. In sum, atomic weapons make bad alliances.

Other new factors affect the direction and intensity of East-West détente. The first is the rapidity of technological change, which further accelerates the nuclear arms race, intensifies the technological gap between East

and West and between the United States and the rest
of the world, and unsettles the American domestic cli-
mate by contributing to student and intellectual unrest. Then there is the population explosion, the con-
cluding phase of decolonization, and the decline of
political stability in the third world. These have conflicting results: on the one hand they create inviting
opportunities for the great powers to extend or revive
their influence in these areas, but on the other they have
convinced Moscow and Washington that in some instances, notably in much of sub-Sahara Africa, this
game isn't worth the candle.

The limits of this paper preclude even the briefest
summary of the history of East-West détente. Nor is
this necessary for its purposes: the post-1953 Soviet-
American détente has been a part of the life of our
times. Its main phases—the Korean Armistice, the 1955
Geneva Summit Conference, the interruptions of it:
the 1956 Polish and Hungarian developments and the
Suez crisis, the second Berlin crisis, and the Cuban missile crisis, the 1963 Test Ban Treaty, the renewed interruptions of the Vietnam war, the Soviet invasion of
Czechoslovakia, the 1967 Israeli-Arab war, and most
recently the renewed signs of Soviet-American détente
—all these are fresh in our memories. Rather, I shall try
to draw from this history some analytical conclusions
relevant to our analysis of the present and future of
East-West relations.

In my view there are two main differences between the American and the Soviet view of détente. The United States generally tends to view détente as an end in itself, as an encouraging step toward peace, arms control, and general international comity. The Soviet Union views it as a political strategy. As Khrushchev said of its Soviet label, "peaceful coexistence," it is the "intensification of the class struggle by all means short of interstate war." Moscow has usually turned toward détente policy because it has suffered a political or military defeat (e.g., in the 1962 Cuban missile crisis). Then, mixed with occasional, carefully timed threats of force or use of force, it maximizes its political benefits and limits its political costs.

During Soviet-American détente the penetration of Soviet influence into the United States-headed NATO alliance and of Western influence into the Soviet-headed Warsaw Pact alliance is easier and more rapid. As we know from East Germany in 1953, Poland and Hungary in 1956, and Czechoslovakia in 1968, the penetration of Western influence into Eastern Europe is seen—correctly—by Moscow as a greater danger to its interests than Washington views what it sees as the penetration of Soviet influence into Western Europe (e.g., with respect to Gaullist policy). Thus Moscow and Washington are confronted by a structural asymmetry, an inevitable inequality, with respect to the effect of détente. The Soviets try to use détente to split the

United States from its allies and reduce its presence and influence in Europe. Conversely, the United States uses détente to attempt to lower Soviet and increase Western influence in Eastern Europe. Since the Soviet position in Eastern Europe can only be maintained by the Red army, Moscow feels compelled to suppress by military intervention what it sees as the bad effects of détente. At the same time, by emphasizing the danger of the arms race and the Middle Eastern crisis, Moscow tries to prevent its military interventions from interrupting the benefits that détente gives it. The United States, conversely, has tried, *inter alia* by profiting from Soviet military interventions, to limit the disintegrative effects of détente within its alliance structure. Washington's policy of peaceful engagement or bridge building was designed to aid liberalization within the Soviet sphere. America's limiting of the Vietnam war was intended in part to prevent it from worsening U.S.-USSR relationships.

Generally speaking, Washington's freedom of movement with respect to détente is much more limited than Moscow's or Peking's. Because of the far greater effect of public opinion on American than on Soviet or Chinese foreign policy, Washington is far less able to reject a Soviet policy of détente than are Moscow and/or Peking to reject such an American policy. This has become even more the case since the length of, and lack of American victory in, the Vietnam war, as well as since the new escalatory cycle in the arms race. Moreover, the main allies of the United States, with the partial exception of conservative circles in West Germany, are even more in favor of détente than Washington, since only through it can their drastic military inferiority be compensated for by increased freedom of maneuver vis-à-vis Washington.

With respect to the Chinese People's Republic, its violent opposition to détente arises from the relative newness and Maoist fanaticism of its regime, from its Taiwan irredenta, and from its conviction that the United States and the Soviet Union are supporting détente in order to combine against Peking and either (like the United States) to crush or (like the Soviet Union) to refuse decisively to aid national liberation struggles. Peking's policy of détente in the mid-1950s (the so-called "Bandung period"), quite effective while it lasted, was submerged at the end of the 1950s by Chinese domestic extremism and international anti-Soviet and anti-American passion. Although Peking still remains strongly opposed to international détente, one should not be misled by its flamboyant and extremist rhetoric: its foreign policies have been in fact low- rather than high-risk in character. Its split with Moscow and America's continued hostility to it combined to further Soviet-American détente. In fact, this has been China's main contribution to détente: parallel Soviet and American hostility to Peking.

One final general point: given the nuclear age and the freezing of territorial boundaries which is one of its products, détente tends to be viewed favorably by status quo powers and unfavorably by unsaturated powers, notably those which have major territorial irredenta: West and East Germany, North and South Korea, North and South Vietnam, Nationalist China. Détente is favorable for those powers, such as the United States, whose external influence spreads primarily through economic expansion: it provides the "open door" which has traditionally favored American business, in China and elsewhere.

*   *   *   *   *   *   *

I turn now to the present world scene. What favors and what opposes détente? What are its future prospects? And what policy conclusions should the United States draw from this analysis?

We have already alluded to some of the major factors encouraging détente and need therefore only mention them here. The first is the fear of nuclear war. The destruction of the second world war would be nothing compared to what a nuclear war would bring. Moreover, the apocalyptic nature of nuclear destruction and the defenselessness of mankind vis-à-vis nuclear missiles have had a deep unsettling effect upon our times. One result has been certainly heightened pressure throughout the world, even in the Soviet Union and

China, for détente. As I have already indicated, this danger, plus the fear by the superpowers of nuclear proliferation, with respect both to raising the danger of nuclear war and lowering the relative power of the two superpowers, pushes Washington and Moscow toward détente in order to slow it down. But its escalation is a factor against détente and will be treated in that context below.

Second, there is the desire, notably at present in the United States but also in the Soviet Union, to transfer funds now spent on military expenditures to more peaceful purposes—here to expenditures for poverty and civil rights programs, in the Soviet Union for housing, roads, private automobiles, and other consumer goods.

Third, the existence of mutual enemies, present and possible, helps to limit the Soviet-American conflict relationship. The most important of these, of course, is China. It is in both the Russian and American national interests, as it has been since both became great powers, that Asia not be dominated by any single power hostile to them. For this reason they were both hostile to Japan in 1941, and for this reason they are both hostile to China today. Peking's purpose is to resume the traditional Chinese hegemonic role in East and Southeast Asia, a purpose made the more fanatical and unyielding by Mao's messianic fanaticism for a world revolution of the underdeveloped, colored peoples against the "Soviet-

American double hegemony," and by the territorial irredenta, the Soviet Maritime Province, Outer Mongolia, and Taiwan, which he is prevented from recovering by Moscow and Washington. Moreover, two other past enemies, Germany and Japan, have been at war with both Russia and America, possess the natural and human resources to become significant thermonuclear powers, and are now both allies of the United States. That Moscow should wish to convince Washington that Bonn and Tokyo are dangerous to them both is quite understandable from the Soviet viewpoint. Washington, however, correctly continues to see Moscow and Peking as its main present rivals. Nevertheless, to the extent that the United States accepts the limitation of its conflict relationship with the Soviet Union, it will almost inevitably pay less attention to the wishes of its West German and Japanese allies—as has been most recently demonstrated by the differences among the three with respect to the non-proliferation treaty, which for the Soviet Union is primarily a further means of preventing West Germany from obtaining a thermonuclear capability.

Fourth, as also has been mentioned above, there is the pressure of its allies on each superpower. This is much more important for the United States than for the Soviet Union, since East European states most closely tied to Moscow, the East Germans and Poles, tend to oppose rather than to favor détente, while those who favor it, like the Czechs, Rumanians, and Yugoslavs, have little influence on Soviet policy or are seen by Moscow as hostile to it. Conversely, the allies closest to Washington, Great Britain and West Germany, favor détente. The former favors it much more than the latter, because of its military weakness, desire for trade with the East, and fear of a resurgent West Germany. The latter is split: West German conservatives only recently and partially changed to support of détente, and then only as a disagreeable necessity, while the German Social Democrats have always supported it. De Gaulle was for détente, *inter alia* in order to lower American influence in Europe, and, optimally, to establish a Franco-Russian condominium there, with an American guarantee but without an American presence. France's internal weakness, the Soviet invasion of Czechoslovakia, and De Gaulle's resignation have ended this dream for the present.

Italy, with the Socialist leader Pietro Nenni as foreign minister, is more pro-détente than ever. The smaller European powers also favor détente. Japan, militarily weak and dependent on foreign trade, is a strong supporter of it. Even Spain and Portugal are becoming less hostile to the Soviet Union, while Greece maintains correct, and Turkey nearly cordial, relations with Moscow.

I now turn to the factors unfavorable to détente. The most enduringly important one is the intractable political issues which have divided Moscow and Washington since the end of World War II. It is now fashionable, on the political left, to rewrite the history of the cold war so as to give Moscow much less, and Washington much more, blame for its inception and course. I find most of those attempts, although sometimes intellectually stimulating to read, unconvincing. What is more important, though, than who started it, is that, in my view, there never really was any chance of avoiding the cold war. The territorial issues between the United States and the Soviet Union in 1945, most of all the division of Germany, traditional Russian policy of becoming the first power in Europe and traditional American policy of avoiding domination of that continent by any hostile power, all reinforced by conflicting ideologies, made it almost inevitable that this essentially structural conflict would break out and persist. This is the basic cause of the conflict relationship which has dominated Soviet-American relations ever since—limited, but certainly not overcome, by détente. The view that either industrialization (or mutual enmity toward China) will produce something like a Soviet-American alliance is certainly not mine; rather, I regard it as "vulgar Marxism."

With respect to the second factor working against détente, the escalation in the nuclear arms race, a less brief treatment is required. This current escalation under way has, in my view, two underlying causes: the paradoxical nature of the military and technological asymmetry between the two superpowers and the new technological developments in the arms race.

The former can be briefly described. The Soviet Union is both sufficiently powerful and determined to reject anything less than military and political parity with the United States, but it is not sufficiently strong to attain parity unless superior United States power is lessened by declining United States will. The Soviet drive for parity—or perhaps: who can tell?—for superiority in deliverable intercontinental thermonuclear capability plus its move toward acquiring a worldwide air and naval intervention capability illustrate the former. The latter is demonstrated by the rising qualitative superiority of United States technology, military and industrial. More recently it has been accompanied by increasing public pressure in the United States for cuts in defense and space expenditures.

The second cause, the new technological developments in the arms race, requires more extensive treatment. These are two: the development by the United States, and presumably in the near future by the Soviet Union as well, of multiple independently-targeted re-entry vehicles (MIRV)—between three and ten such warheads in one ICBM. These new multiple warheads are both less heavy than present ones and above all far more accurate. They thus provide an increase in "assured destruction capability" of a magnitude variously estimated at from ten to fifty times. The second development is the United States anti-ballistic missile system (ABM), which gives major protection to cities and missile sites against a primitive nuclear power (e.g., China) and some (but limited) against the Soviet Union. The essential problem in evaluating it is to estimate its cost-effectiveness with respect to a resultant deployment by Moscow of more offensive missiles, i.e., its escalatory effect on the thermonuclear arms race.

The Soviets, meanwhile, have been rapidly deploying a large-yield but not too accurate missile, the SS-9, by now some 1,200, more than the 1,054 United States land-based ICBMs. The United States still retains its overall strategic superiority, due to its land-based bombers, and the Polaris nuclear submarine fleet, still invulnerable to counterforce attack. (The Soviets are also developing such a fleet.)

Of these two new technological developments, MIRV and ABM, MIRV is potentially destabilizing to a high degree, and ABM can be. First, MIRV's enormous increase in accuracy and therefore in cost-effectiveness marks a major breakthrough from quantity to quality. Indeed, except for the anticipated Soviet response, it could move the United States toward the most de-stabilizing posture of all: a potential first-strike capability. ABM was first deployed by the Soviet Union around Moscow, at a technological level lower than the present proposed United States system. (Indeed, the

United States MIRV was a reply to the Soviet ABM, just as the United States ABM is a reply to the Soviet SS-9.) The new cycle of arms escalation, well under way, leads to suspicion, increased expenditures, and rise of tension on both sides. It has also led to renewed United States and Soviet interest in arms control negotiations on offensive and defensive strategic weapons, which seem about to begin.

This Pandora's box of MIRV and ABM also raises another even more difficult problem: inspection. Since the Soviet Union will not allow on-ground inspection, and since the United States—wisely, in my view—refuses to accept nonverifiable arms agreements with the Soviet Union, both sides have had recourse in recent years to the extremely accurate photographic technology of artificial space satellites. But the qualitative effectiveness of MIRV and ABM cannot be so photographed: the camera cannot see inside the radar and computers of ABM or the warhead of a MIRV missile. True, photography can give some indication of what an ABM system is like, but MIRV effectiveness seems impenetrable to it. Thus both Moscow and Washington will be much more uncertain of each other's strategic capability after MIRV and/or ABM deployment. Both will therefore probably overcompensate for the greater potential error in their estimates. This new built-in escalatory factor will thus further accelerate the arms race.

Two other factors in the conventional military field may worsen U.S.-USSR relations and work against détente: the Soviet drive for long-range naval and air power and the result of the Vietnam war. The first has already posed a potential threat to the United States position in the Mediterranean; if it increases, a further United States naval buildup seems likely. The second is yet uncertain; the result of the fighting and of the battle between Hanoi and Washington for United States public opinion will determine it. The Vietnam war has been cheap and profitable for the Soviet Union as compared to its cost to the United States. If Washington pulls out unilaterally and Hanoi thus wins, Moscow could well thereby be encouraged to indulge in further aid to national liberation struggles. (This would be even more true for Peking.)

The second major factor working against U.S.-USSR détente is the anti-détente policies of some Soviet and American allies. For Moscow this is clearly true of East Germany, North Korea, and North Vietnam; for the United States, West Germany (although less so recently), South Korea, South Vietnam, and Nationalist China. All of these are divided countries and fear that détente will confirm their indefinite partition. Some, however, like the present Bonn government, have come to regard détente as a precondition for improvement of communications with the other half of their country. Most, however, prefer either guerrilla war (Hanoi and

Pyongyang) or relentless crisis diplomacy (East Berlin). Moscow and Washington have not abandoned their pro-détente policies as a result of these extremist pressures, but they have been slower than they otherwise would have been in pushing them.

A third factor which often tends to work against détente is its asymmetrical results, notably in Eastern and Western Europe. As has already been indicated, the West has a structural advantage in this respect, since Moscow is more vulnerable in Eastern Europe than the United States is in Western Europe. The Soviet invasion of Czechoslovakia certainly slowed down Soviet-United States détente. Conversely, Moscow's successes, before it, with General de Gaulle gave both Washington and Bonn some second thoughts about détente in Europe.

A fourth factor is the continuing destabilization in the third world. This creates desires for profit (and fear of profit by one's opponent) in Moscow and Washington—Moscow, for example, in the Middle East, Washington in Indonesia, Ghana, etc. Only when Soviet-United States joint interests in containing China are at stake, as in support of India, can third world destabilization not inhibit toward U.S.-USSR détente.

The Middle East is of all areas of the world probably the one in which a geographically-limited Soviet-American confrontation in the next decade is the most likely, for three reasons. First, it is geographically close to the

Soviet Union, accessible from the Soviet fleet in the Mediterranean, a traditional area of Russian expansionism, and its radical governments inevitably look for Soviet support against Israel. Second, its oil, still vital to Western Europe and Japan, is in part exploited by American corporations, and the United States traditionally supports both Israel and the so-called "conservative" Arab governments. Third, the 1971 withdrawal of the British from the Persian Gulf will create a new power vacuum into which the Soviets are already clearly planning to move.

Thus although a Soviet-United States war over the Middle East is most unlikely, neither superpower can control its allies there. Moreover, the Soviet naval build-up in the Mediterranean has two reasons, both unfavorable to Soviet-United States détente: to increase Soviet political and military influence in the area and to deter the United States Sixth Fleet from again conducting a landing operation, such as in 1958 in the Lebanon, directed against Arab radicalism. In short, then, the Middle East and the strategic arms race will probably be in the 1970s the two major factors working against a Soviet-American détente.

It may seem strange that I have not yet mentioned among the anti-détente factors the one of ideology. After all, Soviet expansionism has historically been stoked by Marxism-Leninism as well as by traditional Russian expansionist tendencies. Conversely, ideological anti-communism greatly heightened the fervor of U.S. cold war opposition to Soviet policies. In the Soviet Union the official Marxist-Leninist ideology is becoming increasingly ossified, a cover for chauvinistic and expansionist tendencies, detested by rebellious intellectuals and seen by restless minorities and East Europeans as a cloak for great Russian chauvinism. Conversely, the conflict with China for leadership in the Communist world is certainly a factor, as Soviet aid to Vietnam has demonstrated, which reintroduces the ideological factor in such a way as to work contrary to U.S.-USSR détente. On balance, however, the Sino-Soviet conflict, as I have already indicated, tends to favor détente, not only because of the parallel U.S.-USSR interest in the containment of China but also because it has increasingly eroded the credibility and unity of the ideology itself. In the United States anti-Communist ideology remains strong, albeit somewhat diminished by détente and Communist disunity.

*   *   *   *   *   *   *

So far relatively little has been said about internal political factors affecting détente: let me turn to them briefly at this point. With respect to the Soviet Union, the last few years have seen a general retrogressive trend in Soviet policy, with respect both to liberalization at home and to détente abroad; and the end is not yet in sight. Intellectual and minority disaffection in the

Soviet Union is now very great, comparable, perhaps, to what existed in the Russian Empire at the end of the nineteenth century. But to date the repressive reaction of the Brezhnev-Kosygin regime in Moscow shows no signs of any failure of authoritarian nerve. On the contrary, Soviet trials, deportations, and labor camp sentences have taken a heavy toll among dissident intellectuals. The fear of the Soviet leadership of the destabilizing effects of the 1968 liberalization in Czechoslovakia on Poland, East Germany, and the Soviet Union itself was probably the primary motive in the Soviet invasion of that unhappy country last August. Moscow has been increasingly fearful of what it sees as the subversive effects of Western, and especially American and West German influence in the Soviet Union and Eastern Europe. This Soviet fear covers a very broad spectrum: the higher level of Western technology, the attractions of the Western consumer-oriented economy, the nonconformist New Left radicalism of Western intellectuals and students, and what Moscow sees as American and West German political plans to "roll back" its influence in Eastern Europe and the third world. Moscow has therefore for the last year been consciously limiting détente with the United States to specific areas, such as the strategic arms race and the Middle East, in order to prevent the United States from again reversing the recent Soviet strategic gains as well as to prevent a Soviet-American military confrontation over, and get

American recognition of Soviet interest in the Middle East. Moscow now seems determined to bar Western influence more effectively from Eastern Europe than before the Czechoslovak invasion and to frustrate the new, détente-oriented West German eastern policies, thus keeping West German influence also out of Eastern Europe and preventing the destabilization of East Germany.

The American domestic scene, to which I now turn, is now dominated by the Vietnam war, black discontent, and student ferment. While I continue to support the strategic objectives which determined the last administration's decision to undertake massive military intervention in South Vietnam, the prevention of domination of East and Southeast Asia by Soviet or Chinese power or both, I think it likely that future historians will judge that President Johnson's reach exceeded his grasp. True, he was pursuing a policy which Presidents Eisenhower and Kennedy had pursued before him. True, the Vietnam war is not yet over and the military results remain unclear. (Indeed, recent reports from Saigon indicate that the United States and South Vietnamese military position has improved somewhat.) Yet the public opposition in the United States to the war, or, more accurately, to its length, casualties, and indecisiveness, opposition which forced President Johnson to political abdication, is probably only in suspense at the moment. Unless, which seems unlikely, the Paris negotiations rapidly move toward settlement, it can be counted upon soon to re-emerge, stronger than ever, against President Nixon.

The Vietnam war has deeply split the American polity. It has led to a massive alienation of intellectuals and students. It has greatly lowered the prestige of the United States abroad, with the partial exception of Southeast Asia. The United States never fought the Vietnam war with full priority for political and social modernization, a policy without which no guerrilla war can be won. In addition, as the Sino-Soviet split became more apparent and deep, the American people have understandably seen the threat of both in Asia somewhat diminished.

From the viewpoint of United States-Soviet détente, however, perhaps the most important result of the Vietnam war, reinforced by widespread understandable and proper increased concern with the defects of our own society, with respect to the poor, the blacks, and the quality of life itself, has been a growing public revulsion centered in, but not confined to, the intellectual, professional, and student classes, about the role of the "military-industrial complex" in American society. This issue falls outside the scope of this paper; suffice it to say here that in my view there is considerable validity in the views of those who regard its power and influence as too great.

From the aspect of Soviet-American détente, the

current rising domestic attack on the "military-industrial complex" can have, depending upon how successful it is, two contradictory effects. On the one hand, insofar as the attack contributes toward a United States political and military posture, notably with respect to strategic arms control negotiations, which is viewed by more moderate elements in the Soviet leadership as relatively forthcoming and lacking in obdurate hostility, it might at least in the short run contribute somewhat to Soviet-American détente. Yet on the other hand, insofar as the attack may result in a significantly lower American defense posture, and especially if the Soviets continue their strategic and conventional escalation of the arms race, it could very well encourage those elements in Moscow—the Soviet military-industrial complex—who are probably even now pressing for the Soviet Union to aim for strategic and conventional military superiority over the United States and for higher risk-taking in such areas of geographic confrontation as the Middle East. To strike here a balance between opportunity and danger is one of the most difficult tasks facing the Nixon Administration.

*   *   *   *   *   *   *

So much for the present; what of the prospects for Soviet-American détente? The only honest answer, in my view, is that they are unclear. There are strong factors working for and against it. Let us therefore try to sketch out the limits within which the continuing cyclical course of détente may move. In the first place, the jointly-felt desire to limit as much as possible the danger of a nuclear confrontation, as well as that of a conventional confrontation, in the Middle East, for example, will almost surely guarantee that some degree of détente will continue to characterize Soviet-American relations. Second, since the current Soviet tendency toward limiting détente out of fear of its destabilizing effects within the Soviet orbit seems likely to persist, Soviet-American détente will not for some time to come reach the level that it did before the invasion of Czechoslovakia. Third, the escalation of the arms race will on balance also probably remain an inhibiting factor in any growth of Soviet-American détente. The same will probably be true with respect to the permanent crisis in the Middle East, although there both Moscow and Washington will continue to reassure each other of their desire to avoid a confrontation. As we move into the 1970s, the rising Soviet worldwide intervention capability will tempt Moscow to use it and may thereby inhibit or at least interrupt détente. Sino-Soviet relations seem likely to remain bad for some time to come. The prospect for immediate improvement in Sino-American relations is also not great, due to Maoist rigidity in Peking and remnants of United States rigidity in Washington. Yet were such improvement to seem probable, Soviet interest in détente with the United States would most likely increase in order to prevent joint Sino-American hostility against the Soviet Union. Japanese influence, which works for détente, will become greater; Western Europe will remain militarily weak, politically divided, and pro-détente; and neither will decisively influence U.S.-USSR relations. In short, Soviet-American relations are likely to remain in the near future what they have been in the recent past: a changing and often contradictory combination of conflict and détente.

*   *   *   *   *   *   *

Given this uncertain forecast, what can and should the United States do about Soviet-American détente? To begin with the minimal and most generally acceptable point, Washington should continue to favor a level of détente with Moscow sufficient to guard against the risk of nuclear war and major conventional military confrontations. (The Soviet Union will most likely favor this also. This alone, as has been pointed out above, makes our reciprocation almost inevitable, but in my view it is desirable as well.)

Second, the United States should combine readiness to relax tensions with maintenance of military strength and credible will to use it at a level such that Moscow's expansionism will continue to be contained. Moscow's turns to détente have historically been a result *inter alia* of successful United States containment, while conversely Moscow's sense of increased strength (e.g., in 1957 with the Sputnik) have led to crises (e.g., the second Berlin crisis in 1958). The old Roman proverb remains valid, *Si vis pacem, para bellum* ("if you wish peace, prepare for war"); and so does Winston Churchill's aphorism, "We arm to parley."

Statements of such general principles are of course easy; the rub comes when they must be put into practice. Let us try to draw some optimum limits of United States maneuver. With respect to the strategic relationship with the Soviet Union, détente will be furthered, and so will United States interests, by an American thermonuclear posture clearly not inferior to the Soviets, and yet not so superior that it might be seen in Moscow as a drive toward a first-strike capability. Parity, because increasingly uninspectable, is no longer a fruitful concept. We should initiate arms negotiations with the Soviet Union, but we should have realistic, because limited, expectations of them. Specifically, the worsening prospects for inspection outlined above make it likely that we can at best hope to get a limitation on missile launchers. (However, the negotiations themselves tend to slow down the arms race.) We should press for mutual agreement not to deploy ABM against cities, where it is destabilizing, but we should not agree upon a prohibition of ABM to defend missile sites, where it is stabilizing. In other words, we should proceed with President Nixon's Safeguard ABM plan, *inter alia* because we cannot anticipate that the Soviets will agree to ABM prohibition entirely. Moreover, we should pursue a vigorous ABM research and development program in the hope that city defense might be developed. We should continue MIRV deployment, gauged to the extent of Soviet deployment as well.

As to Vietnam, we should continue to press our efforts at settlement and should begin some unilateral troop withdrawals, even if Hanoi refuses to reciprocate, in order to convince Saigon that we really mean to end the war. We should pursue the Four Power discussions on the Middle East, not because they are likely to lead to very much but because they help to defuse the danger of a superpower confrontation and may well lower the level of arms shipments to the area, as well as make the Four Powers restrain the Arabs and the Israelis more than they otherwise might. With respect to Japan, potentially our most important single ally, we should rapidly move out of Okinawa and consult with Tokyo fully on our policies toward Moscow and Peking. With respect to Western Europe, in my view President Nixon struck a correct and refreshing note when he indicated during his recent trip that while we continued to be in favor of European unity we had no favorite plan for it, that we did not intend through hostility to France to divide Europe, and that we looked toward a European solution for European problems. Moreover, he wisely stressed his purpose to consult and concert our policies with our European allies before undertaking negotiations with the Soviet Union, something which unfortunately the Kennedy and Johnson Administrations too often did not do. With respect to Eastern Europe, we should intensify our policy of peaceful engagement toward Rumania and Yugoslavia, and treat the invaders of Czechoslovakia with the lack of cordiality which is the least they deserve. As to Cuba, we should be primarily concerned about trying to eliminate the Soviet military presence there and to prevent it being established elsewhere in Latin America.

We must give particular attention to our policies toward Mainland China. There is no reason we should take sides in the Sino-Soviet conflict. True, China has been verbally more hostile to us than Russia has. But Chinese actions have been low-risk in nature; the Soviet Union alone has the power to destroy us; and Khrushchev's emplacement of missiles in Cuba plus the second Berlin crisis show what risks the Soviets are prepared to take if they see inviting opportunities.

It is not in our interest that the Sino-Soviet alliance revive. Rather, for our purposes these two hostile powers should remain more hostile to each other than to us. We should be neutral between them and profit from their mutual hostility. This means, specifically, that we should now begin to adjust our policy toward

Peking toward the kind of limited détente with China which we now have with the Soviet Union, including arms control negotiations, trade and cultural exchange, entry of Peking into the United Nations, and so forth.

Such a revision of our China policy will neither be easy nor will it soon be successful. Mao remains rigidly hostile to us, and we still have the remnants of the "China Lobby" to contend with here at home. But Mao will not live forever and his successors may well moderate their hostility to us. Indeed, their attitude to us, after Mao departs, will be influenced by what we do now while he still rules. We should therefore now outline our vision, as sketched above, of how we hope Sino-American relations would develop. This will lower the risk of war in Asia. It will make our post-Vietnam commitments there easier to bear. Last but certainly not least, it will influence the Soviet Union toward intensifying its détente with us in order to avoid one of its greatest nightmares: a Sino-American alliance against it.

*   *   *   *   *   *   *

The lessons of postwar history seem to me to demonstrate, all too often with frightening clarity, that only such a mixture of power with restraint in its use can guarantee our security. There is, however, one other aspect of our posture toward détente on which I would close: the necessity of a reformulation of our goals in foreign policy in light of the experience of the Vietnam war and of domestic unrest.

It is now fashionable for everyone to say that "of course we cannot be the policeman of the world." True: even if we could, we won't; but that, I think, is not the main point. Rather, we must reconsider our course over the last decade, abroad and at home, in the light of the views of those on the left—largely mistaken, in my view—that America has stumbled, almost unconsciously, into becoming an imperial nation, affluent but unjust to its poor and blacks, repellent to the cream of its youth at home; and abroad, while issuing hypocritical declarations of peace and security, addicted to military intervention to preserve the status quo of wealth and privilege against the revolutionary aspirations of the third world.

To repeat, I consider this line of criticism largely incorrect. It can, however, illumine for us, although in a different light than its authors have intended, what seems to me to have been our major mistake during the past decade. In spite of our seventeenth century heritage of the Puritan insistence on the infinite corruption of mankind, the optimism of the Enlightenment, of the vast, conquered frontier, of our technological triumphs—in short, our unbounded confidence, as we boasted in World War II, that "the difficult we do immediately, the impossible takes a little longer" —have led us into an idealistic, well meaning, but, I submit, counterproductive neo-Wilsonian attempt to make over the world in our own image of peace and stability. The war in Vietnam, we were told, was to be a test case whether national liberation wars could succeed anywhere. Our security, this view maintained, depended upon maintaining stability, the sanctity of international boundaries—in short, to quote the motto on the Great Seal of the United States, the establishment of a "new order of the ages." When applied to Soviet or Chinese advance, true; but our reach for universal stability exceeded our grasp.

What we have lacked, and what our seventeenth century ancestors did not, is a sense of the tragedy, the incompleteness, the disorder, the instability of our times. We will not ally with Moscow against Peking or with Peking against Moscow; on the contrary, we can at best hope for limitation of our long-range conflict relationship with both. General and complete disarmament will not come; arms control will be only partial; the arms race spiral will probably continue. Above all, the third world will become less democratic, more disorderly, more intractable, and more hungry. When as in Vietnam we tried to bring stability, we are by now confronted with the—partially true—accusation that we, as Tacitus said of the Roman conqueror of Britain, "have made a desert and called it peace."

In short, then, we should concentrate our efforts on maintaining our own security, keeping our alliances with developed countries strong, continuing our pursuit of limited détente with Moscow and of beginning it with Peking, and alleviating the hunger, but not guaranteeing the stability of the third world. More than that we should be cautious about undertaking. We should divest ourselves of ideological crusades, either against communism or for democracy. Russia and China are dangerous to us not because they are Communist—their attractiveness as a model continues to decline—but because they are strong and hostile. Castro is dangerous to us because he has made Cuba into a Russian base but not because he calls himself Communist. Rumania and Yugoslavia are Communist but less hostile to us than to Russia; and while Bucharest today is not democratic, neither was it under King Carol.

And while we should not overestimate the extent of ferment in this country, we should not underestimate it either. After all, it is a national shame and an international scandal, in my view, that in the midst of the greatest affluence the world has ever known so many American blacks and poor live in squalor and neglect. Need we be surprised that the ideals of liberalism, tolerance, and charity which we have preached to our children should be taken seriously by many of them? Need we be surprised that American radical youth is not prepared to live by bread alone, or even by automobiles and television, but, rather, seeks a higher, more humane quality in our daily lives than the needless rush of our technology offers them? Indeed it is the very rush of technology itself which produces our youth's often wordless, inchoate desire to revive the pre-industrial ideals of community, of small-group mutual loyalty, of rural neighborliness which so little survive the onrush of the post-industrial age.

True, their reach of the more radical among them also often exceeds their grasp. Too often their revolutionary fervor becomes perverted by violent means into sectarian fanaticism and brutal intolerance. But as we properly maintain the rule of law against the neo-fascist assaults of these sectarian radicals, we should not forget that many of the goals of restless youth are, or ought to be our goals as well to make America a more "green and pleasant land."

American attractiveness as a model for the world, American influence abroad, even American security, all depend on a vital, united nation at home as much as on missiles and foreign bases. The view of tomorrow's rulers of Russia and of China of our nature and our intentions will be an important factor in their attitude toward us. Our security abroad will in part be determined by the quality of what we are and what we do at home. Our foreign policy problems are, as I have tried to show above, difficult but not insoluble. A judicious combination of strength, détente, and self-limitation can go far toward at least containing them in the years to come. The solution of our problems here at home is not only more difficult but also a prerequisite, in my view, for our security. We shall all have our hands full with both.

SECOND LECTURE

WALT W. ROSTOW

I. An Approach to the Question

Is United States-Soviet détente possible? A short answer is: Yes; but it is by no means certain.

It is, perhaps, worth making two further cryptic comments at the beginning. First, détente is defined in Webster's International as a "relaxation of strained relations or tensions" between nations. But to achieve that relaxation between the United States and the USSR may require rather more positive movement towards stable peace than the amiable negativism of the definition would suggest.

Second, the path to peace—like the path to cold war and recurrent confrontation—will not be determined by United States-Soviet relations in the narrow sense: those relations will continue to reflect the changing environment which each nation confronts and how Moscow and Washington deal with that environment as well as with each other.

How United States-Soviet relations, in fact, evolve depends on the outcome of three complex historical processes: first, the process of power diffusion within the Communist world, including the reaction to it of the Soviet Union and Soviet society in the widest sense;

second, the process of power diffusion within the non-Communist world and whether it yields a structure of regional and global order—or chaos; and, third, the capacity of the United States as a society to play the steady but changing role necessary to encourage an outcome of relatively stable peace.

I shall have something to say about each of these processes and possible outcomes.

II. The Communist World

The place to begin is with the Communist vision of a world which, through the dynamics of historical forces, guided, led, and coerced by a "correct" Communist party line, will yield a universal Communist empire. The weight attached to that vision and the manner in which it may now affect the operational behavior of various Communist leaders is open to question. It is even open to question whether Stalin, Khrushchev, and Mao—at their most hopeful and expansive moments—fully "believed" in this vision. But what has been important and remains important is that this image of the tendency of history and of the duty of good Communists with respect to historical forces has imparted a sense of legitimacy to Communists engaged in efforts to expand their power by moving arms and men across international frontiers. And a transformation of this sense of legitimacy in violating international frontiers with movements of arms and men is ultimately involved in progress towards détente and peace.

Against this background—and to understand where we are and the possibilities and dangers ahead—it is useful to recall the shape and rhythm of what we have experienced in the past generation.

There was Stalin's thrust of 1946-51 (in association with Mao, from 1949); Khrushchev's of 1958-62; and, finally, the offensive conducted over recent years by Mao and those who accepted his activist doctrines and policies with respect to so-called "wars of national liberation."

Starting in early 1946, Stalin consolidated into Communist states those countries of Eastern Europe where Soviet troop positions provided leverage, while pressing hard against Iran, Greece, Turkey, and then, via the Communist parties, in Italy and France. His effort reached its climax in the Berlin blockade of 1948-49.

The West did not defend the hard-won wartime agreements on political freedom in Eastern Europe but responded with the Truman Doctrine, the Marshall Plan, and the creation of NATO as Western Europe came under threat. A stalemate developed after the success of the Berlin airlift in 1949.

As this duel in the West proceeded, Stalin, working through the Cominform, launched an offensive in the East which can roughly be dated from Zhdanov's speech of September 1947. It involved guerrilla warfare in Indochina, Burma, Malaya, Indonesia, and the Philippines. And after the Chinese Communists came to power in November 1949, the offensive in Asia reached its climax with the invasion of South Korea. It ended in May 1951, with the successful United Nations defense at the 38th parallel against a massive assault by the Chinese Communists, although costly fighting continued for two further painful years.

From the opening of truce talks in the summer of 1951 to the launching of the first Soviet Sputnik in October 1957, there emerged what passes in postwar history for a relatively quiet interval. It was, of course, interrupted by the Suez and Hungarian crises in 1956; but these resulted less from the tensions of the cold war than from the dynamics of change within the non-Communist and Communist worlds, respectively. During this time, the Soviet Union was mainly engaged in its post-Stalin redispositions—political, economic, and military.

Meanwhile, Communist China turned primarily to tasks of domestic development. Only in Indochina did local conditions favor major Communist momentum; but the North Vietnamese settled at Geneva in 1954 for half the victory they had sought.

Khrushchev's domestic changes represented a significant softening of Stalin's harsh regime—and for Soviet citizens, historic gains. His foreign policy style was different, too, and, in its way, more flexible. Nevertheless, considerable ambitions remained embedded in

Moscow's foreign policy. And with the launching of Sputnik, a new phase of attempted Communist expansion got under way.

By that time Khrushchev had consolidated unambiguous control over the machinery of the Soviet government as well as over the Communist party. He looked to the exploitation of two new facts on the world scene: first, the emerging Soviet capacity to deliver thermonuclear weapons over long distances as a means of forcing the West to make limited diplomatic concessions; second, the marked acceleration of nationalism and modernization in Asia, the Middle East, Africa, and Latin America, yielding an environment of endemic turbulence on those continents.

It was in this post-Sputnik period that Moscow laid down its ultimatum on Berlin; the Communist party in Hanoi announced it would undertake to revive guerrilla warfare in South Vietnam; Castro took over in Cuba; and Soviet military and economic aid arrangements were extended to increase their leverage not only in the Middle East, where the process had begun earlier, but also in Indonesia and elsewhere. It was then that Mao announced, "The East Wind is prevailing over the West Wind"; and, in that spirit, he initiated in 1958 the crisis in the Taiwan Straits.

There was a good deal of opportunistic enterprise rather than a majestic grand design in all this; but it was clearly a phase of Communist confidence and attempted forward movement.

In 1961-62, Khrushchev's offensive was met by the West as a whole at Berlin; and a further dramatic test of nuclear blackmail was faced down by President Kennedy in the Cuba missile crisis. For the time being at least, that latter crisis answered a question which had greatly engaged Khrushchev: whether the Free World would surrender vital interests through diplomacy, under the threat of nuclear war.

The answer to the second question—concerning the ability of the West to avert successful Communist exploitation of the inherent vulnerability of the developing area—had to be given at many points by many devices:

—In Laos, by an evident determination to frustrate a Communist takeover, yielding the Geneva Accords of 1962;

—In Vietnam, by President Kennedy's decision in December 1961 to enlarge our support for the South Vietnamese;

—In Africa, by the whole cast of European and American approaches to the new African nations; and, in particular, support for the United Nations effort in the Congo;

—In Latin America, by the isolation of Castro's Cuba and the launching of the Alliance for Progress.

By the end of the Cuba missile crisis in the autumn of 1962, the momentum had largely drained out of

Khrushchev's post-Sputnik offensive; but Moscow's move towards moderation, symbolized by the negotiation of the atmospheric test ban treaty in 1963, had no echo in Peking.

The Sino-Soviet split was gravely aggravated after the Cuba missile crisis and became increasingly overt as recriminations were exchanged and inter-party documents revealed.

The Chinese Communists sought to seize the leadership of the Communist movement, notably in the developing areas, and to unite it with the radical nationalists of Asia and Africa. They thrust hard against Soviet influence within Communist parties on every continent, fragmenting some of them; sought to bring Castro aboard; moved boldly, overplaying their hand, in Africa; probably played some role in triggering the attempted Communist takeover in Indonesia; and struck an aggressive pose during the Indo-Pakistani war of 1965. As a result of the problems they created, the Afro-Asian conference at Algiers in 1965 never materialized.

At one point after another this Chinese Communist offensive in the developing world fell apart, leaving the war in Vietnam as perhaps the last major stand of Mao's doctrine of guerrilla warfare. That war was revived by Hanoi on a new basis, with the introduction of regular North Vietnamese forces, in the wake of political disintegration in Saigon in 1963-64.

There is a certain historical logic in this outcome.

For the better part of a decade, an important aspect of the struggle within the Communist movement between the Soviet Union and Communist China had focused on the appropriate method for Communist parties to seize power. The Soviet Union had argued that the crossing of frontiers with arms and men should be kept to a minimum and the effort to seize power should be primarily internal. They argued that it was the essence of "wars of national liberation" to expand Communist power without causing major confrontation with the United States and other major powers. The Chinese Communists defended a higher risk policy; but they were militarily cautious themselves. Nevertheless, they urged others to accept the risks of confrontation with United States and Western strength, against which the Soviet Union warned.

Although Hanoi's effort to take over Laos and South Vietnam proceeded from impulses which were substantially independent of Communist China, its technique constituted an important test of whether Mao's method would work even under the optimum circumstances provided by the history of the area. As General Giap has made clear, Hanoi is conscious of this link: "South Viet Nam is the model of the national liberation movement in our time . . . if the special warfare that the United States imperialists are testing in South Viet Nam is overcome, this means that it can be defeated everywhere in the world." [1]

So far as the Soviet Union is concerned, what we have seen since the Cuba missile crisis and the Khrushchev removal is a policy increasingly motivated by anxiety and concern rather than hope and vision of ideological satisfaction. There was an authentic exuberance about Khrushchev's vision of the future. He may not have been so sure that nuclear blackmail would work; although he gave it a good and mortally dangerous try. But he did believe—as nearly as we can guess—that the Soviet Union would soon catch up with the United States in economic performance. He did believe—as nearly as we can guess—the developing world would prove a promising terrain for Communist expansion.

But since 1962 Soviet economic prospects resumed a more Russian cast; that is, of a society moving forward at a conventional rate but lagging, as traditionally, the West. China has become once again in Soviet policy and in the minds of the Russian peoples a problem and an anxiety—not the vindication of an ideological dream. The developing regions of the world—even the Middle East, the most proximate and promising—have demonstrated a capacity to go their own way, following a variety of non-Communist patterns in their economic, social, and political life, motivated by a sturdy nationalism.

Finally, of course, Stalin's empire in Eastern Europe,

step by step, has shown an assertiveness which has forced Moscow to put aside the question of how it could be used as the base for a westward thrust and has raised again an old Russian question: How can Eastern Europe be managed so that it is not a threat to the security of the Soviet Union?

The movement of history outside the Soviet Union, then, has involved for Moscow a reassertion of the power of nationalism in ways which have imposed steady attrition on the concept of an ideologically united global empire. And within the complex equation which has related Russian nationalism and ideology since the revolution,[2] events have forced a gradual elevation of nationalism in Soviet life and policy.

Moscow still spends $300 million per annum to keep an awkward Castro regime going in Cuba; it played an adventurist game in the Middle East before the June 1967 war; it is pushing outward still in the Mediterranean in an assertion of national power. The old devil is still there. But it is a remarkable event when Soviet ambassadors call upon the Foreign Offices in the major Western trading nations of the world and urge them to limit their sales of sensitive equipment to Communist China. It is also a remarkable moment when a modest degree of nationalism and liberalism in Czechoslovakia stirs anxieties so great that the Soviet Union is prepared to pay a heavy price for even a short-term damping of what are judged to be dangerous trends.

The diffusion of nationalism and nationalist assertiveness within the Communist world is a discomfiture to Communist ideology and Soviet ambitions; but it by no means guarantees, automatically, détente or peace.

Détente—or movement towards peace—must be based on something more positive than merely Soviet fears on its eastern and western borders.

It is wholly possible that Soviet movement in Czechoslovakia resulted from a convergence of concerns that the Warsaw Pact might disintegrate; East Germany might not hold politically; that the Ukraine might be infected by the Czechoslovak disease; and that Soviet liberals might take the goings on in Prague as the benchmark for behavior within the Soviet Union. The Soviet concern about China is for a nation of 700 million, whose leaders are stirring memories of Czarist acquisition of Siberia, armed with nuclear weapons, and a great, if yet unfulfilled, capacity for technical and economic modernization. That is a heavy dose of anxiety for any group of political leaders to bear. And it could lead us not to détente but to reaction of fear and violence—to greater danger rather than to less.

Our experience of United States-Soviet relations in the period of Soviet defensiveness (since, say, the Cuba missile crisis) is not unhopeful; but it does not give us a basis for sure confidence about the future. By painstaking hard work on both sides, we achieved an Atmospheric test ban treaty; intensive collaboration on the non-proliferation treaty; agreement to go forward with strategic missile talks; a consular convention; a civil air agreement; the outer space treaty and the astronauts agreement; cultural exchanges; some slight expansion in United States law and regulation governing East-West trade. The bulk of this progress took place—at President Johnson's stubborn initiative—despite the believed constraints imposed on United States-Soviet relations by the war in Vietnam.

There are seven factors, I believe, which will determine whether the diffusion of power within the Communist world leads further in the direction of stable peace—and true détente—or to an historical phase of further danger and disruption.

First, whether the United States and the Soviet Union enter into a deep and protracted dialogue on the nuclear arms balance. In material terms, what is at stake is the scale of allocations in both countries to military expenditures over the next decade and generation. But of at least equal importance are two secondary consequences of the dialogue. It will, in the first instance, set the atmosphere in which the non-proliferation treaty will be examined in the governments and parliaments of the nations of the world whose assent is critically important for the treaty; that is, Japan, Australia, India, Israel, Germany, Italy, Brazil, and Argentina. It will be much easier for these nations to take this major step if the United States and the Soviet Union are seized, with evident seriousness, of the problem of slowing down the bilateral nuclear arms race.

In addition, the kind of dialogue required to emerge with either informal or formal agreement between the United States and the Soviet Union could lead to a deeper mutual understanding of military purposes on both sides and to a higher degree of stability in United States-Soviet relations.

Second, whether agreement can be reached to defuse the recurrent tension over Berlin and Germany and start even a slow moving process in Central Europe that could lead in time to a resolution of the German problem. Behind any such process must be a willingness of the Soviet Union to see change—even slow change—in the political life of East Germany and a widening of the web of ties between the two parts of Germany. European security understandings, without ameliorative political movement in the heart of Central Europe, are likely to prove illusory.

Third, a continuation of the slow, uncertain movement towards United States-Soviet parallelism in Asia and the Middle East. For a complex of reasons, related to Soviet policy towards China and a recognition of its own limited capacity to influence the course of events in Asia, there has developed a mixture of United States-Soviet rivalry and parallelism in South Asia and, to a degree, even, in Southeast Asia. This could lead to a

situation where Moscow was content to pursue its
political and economic interests in that region, in a general environment of military stability. Should this trend
develop and persist, an increasingly important area—
embracing two-thirds of humanity—might be permitted to evolve and gradually find areas of cooperation
within itself which would give a critical element of
stability to the world environment and to the environment of United States-Soviet relations.

With respect to the Middle East, the almost two years
which have passed since the war of June 1967 have
yielded a slow and laborious shift from United States-
Soviet confrontation, at the time of the hot-line exchanges, to the possibility, at least, of limited parallelism
of purpose. In this least structured and most volatile of
regions, a good deal hinges on the growth of a conviction in Moscow that the risks of uncontrollable explosion outweigh the possible advantages of deeper Soviet
intrusion and extension of power, and on the growth
in the Middle East of an awareness that they will find
neither dignity nor progress until they turn to regional
cooperation.

*Fourth, within the Soviet Union an increasingly ex-
plicit and solid acceptance of the doctrine that Moscow's ideological interests can only safely be pursued
by means short of the use of military force across international frontiers.* As noted above, in the protracted
debate with Communist China in the late 1950s Moscow

took the view that wars of national liberation must be conducted by means which would not lead to major military confrontation with the United States. Pragmatically, that rule of Soviet policy has thus far held: in Berlin, in the Cuba missile crisis, and even in the Middle East. Soviet military doctrine, on the other hand, and Soviet force structures have moved in a direction which would be consistent with a United States-Soviet clash, short of nuclear war. The prognosis, therefore, for Soviet policy with respect to the use of force in relation to its ideological objectives, is uncertain. The outcome is likely to be determined by the military and political environment the Soviet Union confronts, rather than by the abstract triumph of one doctrinal view over another.

Fifth, the future of the Soviet society. Since Stalin's death, there has been a limited but significant degree of liberalization in Soviet society. The secret police are a less arbitrary and personalized instrument of government. The forced labor camps have been significantly curtailed although they still flourish. Executive power is somewhat more diffused at the top of the structure. Within fluctuating limits—now rather narrow—there has been some debate, on some issues, touching the future of Soviet society. The old humane traditions of Russian culture have found at least sporadic expression in poetry, novels, and, occasionally, in views about domestic and international policy. But the Russians, as a people, have exhibited little gift for transforming their politics towards the more modern, stable, democratic basis which, no doubt, most people who live in the Soviet Union would like. There is something frustrating—as well as moving—in Solzhenitsyn's gallant figures of *The First Circle*, who hold to their personal integrity under tragic circumstances, but reflect no capacity to think through the problem of how, starting from where history has placed them, they could build a political life and institutions which would better conform to their values. One senses that Soviet liberals have fallen into the classic nineteenth century counterpoint of protest and private assertion against autocratic rule, but have not resumed the concrete thought and effort towards government by the consent of the governed, which marked the early years of this century.

And so the fate of liberal tendencies in Soviet society remains in question; but this issue will also affect the outcome on the world scene.

The future of the Soviet economy will also have a part to play.

It was possible in the late 1950s to predict that the heavy industry complex, which was the basis of the Soviet growth in the 1930s and the first postwar decade, would decelerate and damp the Soviet rate of growth in the 1960s.[3] That deceleration has occurred. The future of the Soviet growth rate hinges substantially on a decision to turn the Soviet industrial machine in the directions to which the Soviet consumer—like his counterpart in Japan, Western Europe, and North America—evidently desires; that is, the diffusion of the automobile and the whole complex of suburban housing, durable consumers goods, roads, and supporting services that go with this phase of economic and social development. The coming into production of the Fiat plant in the early 1970s may indicate that the Soviet leadership at last has decided to accept the complex costs and changes that go with the automobile age. There is no automatic connection between the domestic economy and foreign policy in a regime like that which rules the Soviet Union. On the other hand, we know from the experience of other nations that movement into the automobile age and all its works has profound social and political consequences which are likely to absorb Soviet energies for a time and make a little less likely, rather than more likely, an adventurous policy abroad.

Sixth is the outcome of the debate and struggle within mainland China. With Mao we have observed an effort unique in modern history—indeed, an effort for which it is difficult to find parallels in history: the grandfather evoking his grandchildren to defeat his children. The children, in this case, are the pragmatic generation of soldiers and technicians who emerged in post-1949 China, who wished to get on with the unfulfilled task of modernizing that old and remarkable civilization. Mao perceived that the consequences of this process would lead China towards a pragmatic and increasingly moderate regime in both its domestic and foreign dispositions. He used his powers in the 1960s to try to stem the tide, as he saw it, via the Cultural Revolution. He produced an economy whose production in 1968 only matched that of a decade earlier; but an economy that contained within it a nuclear weapons complex amidst continuing poverty and relative industrial and agricultural stagnation. There is so much unique about the story of China's modernization that one can only predict with diffidence. But whether mainland China turns, in the years ahead, to a more conventional effort at modernization and whether it develops less pathological relations with the rest of Asia, the Soviet Union and the United States, are, evidently, important variables in United States-Soviet relations.

The seventh factor, of course, is whether the non-Communist world does or does not present opportunities and temptations for Soviet expansion and adventure in the time ahead. The transition of the Soviet leadership to a world where it seeks its satisfactions abroad, essentially through its role as a great but not dominating national state—using its influence, along with others, to organize and defuse an international environment which is judged potentially more threatening than promising to Soviet interests—is a hard transition. For the foreseeable future, we must assume that it is a reluctant choice; and that forces will continue to exist in Moscow which will move towards an expansion of power and influence—even by military means—if the non-Communist world provides opportunity.

III. The Non-Communist World

What kind of an environment is the non-Communist world likely to present to Moscow and Peking as this precarious transition proceeds?

The postwar world took its initial shape from a series of *ad hoc* decisions by the United States to move into vacuums of power which, if filled by Communists, would have shifted the balance of power in Europe and in Asia decisively against us. And, when challenged to the south by the emergence of Castro, the United States took steps, within and outside the Organization of American States, to limit the Communist incursion into the Western Hemisphere, a policy which also shaped United States action during the Cuba missile and Dominican crises.

But starting with Western Europe, the United States began to execute a policy which would convert its initial, reactive defensive commitments into more stable structures which promised, over the long run, reduced United States responsibility on the world scene.

The most substantial expression of this policy has

been an encouragement of regionalism which began, of course, in Western Europe.

Essentially, the movement towards Western European unity recognized three facts:

1. As many Western European leaders looked ahead, starting from the devastation of the second world war and the acute dependence on the United States of the postwar days, they reached out for a method of organization which would give them a larger voice in their own destiny.

2. They perceived, however, that in military, economic, and other matters, a measure of interdependence with the United States would be required for the indefinite future.

3. They accepted the fact that the nation-state— even nation-states of fifty million commanding the best in modern science and technology—could not deal effectively either with the United States as a partner or with the scale of the problems which were emerging on the world scene, whether East-West or North-South.

Western European regionalism was conceived by Europeans as a method for solving this three-sided dilemma. And it had the steady support of the United States which, in 1947, made—and has sustained to this day—a conscious decision that a strong, unified Western Europe was more to its long-run interest than fragmented but less capable European partners.

In the first postwar generation, Western European

unity moved forward substantially, goaded by the Soviet threat but inhibited by an understandable reluc-
tance to surrender deeply rooted national concepts.
Today, despite evident and grave problems, that movement is still alive and active—although effectively frustrated from Paris. As one contemplates the agenda for
the coming generation, as nearly as it can now be
defined, the case remains valid, strengthened by evidence that it is difficult to absorb and apply certain
types of new technology without investments in research and development and markets beyond the reach
of nations of fifty million. Western Europe is unlikely
to make the maximum contribution that it could make
to the tasks of security, human welfare, reconciliation,
and institution-building in the world community unless
it continues to move towards unity.

Meanwhile, in the course of the 1960s, forces similar
to those which initiated economic regionalism in Western Europe began to take hold in other parts of the
world, notably in Latin America, Africa, and, most
recently, in Asia.

Latin American unity is an old dream, dating from
the days of Bolivar. It has taken on a new vitality as
Latin Americans have moved from the first stage of
their industrialization, the production of consumers
goods in substitution for imports, to the growth of
medium and heavy industry. In terms of stages of
growth, the more advanced countries of Latin Amer-

ica—Mexico, the southern regions of Brazil, and Argentina, for example—are emerging from take-off and moving towards technological maturity. In Mexico, at least, that transition has been made successfully, although throughout Latin America industrialization is hobbled by an overly protective system which has diminished competition, efficiency, and full utilization of capacity. Powerful vested interests are embedded in those national protective systems.

But, as the Latin Americans move into industries of higher and more sophisticated technology, they are beginning to try to overcome this heritage of take-off. They feel acutely the constriction of national markets and the irrationality of building steel, automobile, chemical, and other industries on a national basis, behind high tariff barriers. They are also being pushed towards economic integration by an awareness that their traditional exports are unlikely to earn the foreign exchange needed for their further development—that they must cultivate industrial exports; but at the present time they believe they must go through a transitional stage of regional protectionism before they can emerge with competitive efficiency on the world scene.

Meanwhile, the Central American Common Market has demonstrated that countries at a much earlier stage of development can profit greatly from a common market arrangement—a lesson worth the serious attention of Africa, the Middle East, and Southeast Asia.

Finally, the Latin Americans are beginning to look inward from the coastal cities, which historically have been the bases for their modernization. They are beginning to recognize expanding needs and possibilities of international collaboration in developing the inner frontiers of South America.

These convergent and palpable economic forces, making for economic cooperation and integration, are supported by a sense—not unlike that which continues to motivate the European unity movement—that, in the world of the present and the future, the voice of Latin America will be strengthened vis-à-vis the United States and other large powers, to the extent that Latin Americans can find common ground and common policies.

It is natural, therefore, that, despite great resistance and frustration, thoughtful Latin Americans should focus energy and attention on the tasks of economic integration.

In Western Europe and Latin America, those pressing towards unified action could build on substantially common traditions. But in Asia, history has offered a less promising initial base. Nevertheless, we have seen in the past four years a quite remarkable surge of regional enterprise in Asia.

From South Korea to Australia, from Japan to Singapore, there are solid and particular national reasons why the nations of Asia and the Pacific should begin to group together in mutual support. These underlying considerations were strengthened by the American commitment of major forces in Vietnam in 1965, which has given to the region confidence that it has a future to design.

As in Europe and Latin America, the initial expression of this movement has been in the form of economic institutions. It remains to be seen how the encouraging political impulses which underlay the Asian and Pacific Council and the Association of Southeast Asia will evolve.

In Africa, too, one can detect beginnings, at least, of the same mixture of economic and political impulses that have led to regionalism elsewhere. The Organization of African Unity has existed since May 1963. Despite political schisms, both regional and ideological, the OAU undertook to deal with two substantial African disputes—Somalia and Ethiopia, and Morocco and Algeria—thus avoiding the intervention of extra-African powers. It has struggled, with the same motivation, to find the terms for ending the tragic civil war in Nigeria. On the economic side, the African Development Bank has been launched, and subregional economic communities are being formed in East and West Africa as a result of planning by the United Nations Economic Commission for Africa. Most of Africa, as noted earlier, is in a pre-industrial stage, building slowly the preconditions for take-off. It makes good sense to try to create the essential physical and institutional infrastructure, in this pliant early phase of development, on a regional and subregional basis. This was a major consideration that led to the reshaping of the American aid program for Africa in 1966, to give greater emphasis to multinational cooperation.

As the evolution of the movement towards Western European unity indicates, the building of regionalism is a long, slow process. At every stage the case for moving forward must overcome the inherent attraction and inertia of staying with familiar national modes of operation. Moreover, regionalism is no substitute for building solid national structures. Nevertheless, the next generation is likely to see real, if irregular, progress towards regional cooperation, because the political and economic impulses which underlie it are compelling. Regional cooperation—within a framework of global collective security and common efforts in development—is likely to grow, as it must, if the desires of men and governments to take a larger hand in their own destiny are to be reconciled with the inadequacies of the nation-state, on the one hand, and the imperatives of interdependence, on the other.

For the United States, this move towards regionalism has a particular meaning. We were drawn into world responsibility after the second world war by the need to fill certain vacuums of power. The cost of not helping in Greece, Turkey, Western Europe, Korea, and elsewhere, was self-evident; and it was judged, case by case, to outweigh the burden of engagement. But post-war America was not interested in building a network of satellites. It looked forward eagerly to the earliest time when other nations could stand on their own feet and deal with us as partners in as safe and orderly and progressive a world community as we all could achieve.

Regionalism—in Western Europe and elsewhere—has thus commended itself to the United States as a way of permitting us to shift away from the disproportionate bilateral relations inherent in a large power working with smaller powers.

We see in regionalism a way *not* of returning to isolationism but of leaving the nations of the various regions to do as much for themselves as they can—and more with the passage of time—while preserving the ties of interdependence where they are judged on both sides to be in the common interest.

In a speech at New Orleans, on September 10, 1968, while warning against isolationism, President Johnson articulated the doctrine that underlay this systematic effort:

> We have always hoped and believed that as our friends and allies grew in strength, our burden would grow less lonely. We have been moving over the last few years toward a long-term position in which the United States would be able to assume its responsibility in enterprises of common concern, but our partners would be able to assume theirs. . . .

I believe the day will soon come—which we have been building toward for 20 years—when some American President will be able to say to the American people that the United States is assuming its fair share of responsibility for promoting peace and progress in the world, but the United States is assuming no more or no less than its fair share.

And so the American task has become to use our margin of influence to encourage abroad what we have always set as our target at home; namely, the effective organization of diffuse centers of power and authority.

Under President Johnson this objective was pursued as a conscious alternative—somewhere between continued direct over-involvement and a return to isolationism. It governed his approach to monetary affairs, trade, and aid, as well as regionalism.

Should this policy succeed, it would confront the Soviet Union with an environment of increasingly diffuse but sturdy authority in Asia, Africa, and Latin America, as well as in Europe—an environment calculated to discourage rather than encourage military and ideological adventure.

It is a pattern of policy, however, that depends greatly on what nations, other than the United States, do. For example, the outcome depends in part on whether Western Europe, post-De Gaulle, resumes the road towards effective unity, including a bringing of the United Kingdom into European institutions; for it is very unlikely that a Europe still fragmented and bedeviled with Gaullist nationalism, will be able to play a global role on a fair-shares basis.

It depends on whether the Latin Americans in the decade ahead will prove capable of overcoming the heritage of protectionism, monopoly, and fragmentation so that it can move forward to the full economic and social modernization it seeks.

It depends on whether the conflict in the Middle East can be peacefully resolved and that region can begin to find, through regional cooperation and organization, a basis for dignity, which would also limit the capacity for external powers to continue to intrude.

It depends on the outcome in Vietnam, the stability of that outcome, and, particularly, on the willingness of Asian nations, such as Japan and Indonesia, to assume a serious responsibility for the monitoring of the frontiers of Laos and Vietnam, whose violation has been the proximate cause of the terrible war.

And it depends, finally, on the ability of the United States, as a society, to continue to play a role which, if, hopefully, diminished, will still be the critical margin.

IV. The United States: The Critical Margin

The kind of loose federal structure which has emerged *ad hoc* within the non-Communist world will continue to depend for its viability on the United States for several clear—even technical—reasons.

The first is the continued nuclear role implicit in

United States support for a non-proliferation treaty. The non-proliferation treaty is not, as it is sometimes viewed, a United States-Soviet negotiation or an exercise in "bridge building." It is a constitutional arrangement proposed to the world, of the greatest significance for its future political and security structure. The proposition being put to the world's parliaments is that they deny themselves the ambiguous option of a national nuclear weapons capability and seek their security through collective means based on existing—mainly United States—commitments. There have been no public postures more misleading than those of certain United States senators who simultaneously advocated the non-proliferation treaty and urged United States withdrawal from commitment in Vietnam as well as rapid troop withdrawals from NATO. If we are to have a world of non-proliferation—and it is to our interest that it be so—we shall have it only if men in Europe, Asia, and elsewhere, are confident that the United States security commitments will remain viable. This does not mean that United States force structures overseas need remain forever at their present levels. It does not mean that other nations can or should regard their security problems as a matter for the United States to handle virtually alone. It does mean that the American security guarantee should remain credible where it has been given.

Behind this proposition is an aspect of United States

policy rarely articulated. No American President is likely to permit another nation the right to commit the United States to risks of nuclear war without American assent. This means that development of additional national nuclear capabilities, accompanied by the claim of a sovereign right to fire them, will inevitably dilute the United States security commitment. It is an awareness of this fact of life—along with others—which makes thoughtful men abroad draw back from the easy temptation of proceeding to produce a national nuclear capability. A fragmented world of many nuclear powers would be, therefore, a world in which the United States—even contrary to basic interests—would be impelled in the direction of isolationism. It would also be a world in which—with this fact apparent—certain nuclear powers might be tempted to revive again the threat of nuclear blackmail against lesser nuclear powers.

In short, as nearly as one can perceive the alternatives for the United States and the rest of the world, a nonproliferation treaty makes sense. But there follows from it significant, abiding United States responsibilities.

Second, quite aside from the nuclear question, the United States military, political, and economic role will remain a critical margin, even though we have the right to hope and believe that other nations will assume a higher proportion of the task of shaping their own destiny.

The United States margin of influence and responsibility will, of course, vary from time to time and vary with the regions of the world. We have one kind of task in doing what we can to encourage Latin American economic and physical integration; if things go well, a lesser task—but an important one—in helping and encouraging the Africans as they move forward in cooperation towards their first sustained phase of industrialization; a third—and evidently central—continuing task in NATO; and a quite different role in Asia and the Pacific as we see Vietnam through to the end and do what we can to encourage a surge of vitality and cooperative enterprise in the new Asian institutions of regional cooperation.

These are tasks which lie within our objective capabilities, if the nations and regions of the non-Communist world continue to share the underlying proposition on which they rest; namely, that they are prepared to assume enlarged responsibilities but desire also to retain essential links of interdependence with the United States.

The ultimate question is likely to be whether the United States, as a society, can play its subtle but essential part in this transformation—knowing when to pull back, when to hold steady—and to do so without the stimulus of brute challenge, but never forgetting the latent dangers that will persist. Is an America beset with searching domestic difficulties, likely to understand

and take seriously this kind of historical process? The United States is now beginning to confront the ultimate question which economic and social progress poses—can societies sustain their vitality, their sense of purpose, an awareness of their vital interests in a protracted environment of mass affluence?

On America's answers to these questions—more than any other—the future of détente depends.

V. Conclusion

If one brings together the factors which constitute the equation which will determine the future of détente and the movement to peace, one must conclude that the outcome is problematical. With respect to the Soviet Union, the environment of the Communist bloc, interplaying with the dynamics of Soviet society, could yield gradual acceptance of the view that Russia's primary mission is to build a world environment that will be safe for Russia. One can conceive of Soviet leaders and Soviet citizens finding their satisfactions in this task, combined with the conversion of Soviet society to a more affluent and liberal way of life. But there is nothing inevitable about this outcome—an outcome that involves for serious Communists a radical transformation of their image of themselves and the world about them.

A Russia under increasing pressure from forces generated in China and Eastern Europe will be an increasingly fearful Russia; and the combination of fear and great military power in hand is a dangerous combination.

As for the non-Communist world, rather remarkable progress has been made in conventional economic and social terms and a rather hopeful understanding has emerged that if independent nations are to fashion their own destiny in the contemporary world, they must do so through cooperation—regional and global. All this has yielded institutions and policies which have promise. But even in Western Europe the promise is yet to be fulfilled. And there remains in each of these regions a capacity not merely for continued progress and enlarged cooperation but for setbacks and disintegration.

And, finally, there is the question of whether the United States has the historical memory somewhere within it to recall what has happened since the presidential election of 1916 when a man was chosen on the slogans: "Too proud to fight" and "He kept us out of war," only to face, the next spring, the reality of unrestricted submarine warfare in the Atlantic—a switch in posture repeated again and again over the past half century.

We have managed to come this far in the twentieth century, living by Dr. Johnson's proposition: "When a man knows he is to be hanged in a fortnight, it concentrates his mind wonderfully." That is how we reacted in 1940-41, 1947, 1950, and 1965—as well as in 1917.

The hopeful outcome to the equation of détente requires more of the United States than that. It requires a nation whose leadership and people will hold steadily to a consensus that the only long-run safety for its children and grandchildren lies in building a stable world order which was destroyed in 1914 and never replaced; understands that, at great cost and travail to many peoples, we have come some distance towards that goal; that there is a road to peace ahead, but it is rocky and long; and that whatever other problems we face and shall face, it is our interest and duty to follow that road.

REBUTTALS

WILLIAM E. GRIFFITH

To comment on the paper by my old friend and former colleague Walt Rostow is not an easy task, for several reasons. In the first place, he is not only a historian but a historical source—a double distinction I do not share. Second, over the years we have more often agreed than disagreed about the shape of the world and what posture the United States should take toward it. In particular, we were, I remember, both for the bombing of North Vietnam before it began—a fact in my case I feel compelled to lay on the table before I say anything more about our Vietnam embroilment. Third, in the largest sense, it seems to me, our differences, as evidenced in our two papers, reflect at least as much a difference in temperament as in more purely intellectual attitudes. He is more of an optimist than I, and I more of a pessimist than he—about the state of the world and about what the United States can and should do about it. Now this may primarily reflect my Welsh Calvinist background; but as a member of the academic guild, I am required to look for an objective view of where we are; how we got there, and how we can get out.

In what respect am I more pessimistic than he? First, about the third world. My reaction to his optimism about regionalism there, notably in Latin America and Africa, may perhaps best be characterized by Goethe's aphorism: "I hear the message, I just can't believe it." To begin with Africa, his worst—and my best case, what do we see? Military coups, bloody civil war in Nigeria, rising power of the White Redoubt to the south, chronic guerrilla war in the Portuguese colonies, the frustrated African "liberation movements" increasingly turning to Soviet aid. Must one not fear that Africa will be for the late twentieth century what Central America was for the nineteenth, and what Haiti is today? As for Latin America, again I cannot share Professor Rostow's optimism: the population explosion alone seems to me to preclude it, and the rising anti-Americanism of such regimes as Peru, arising in part from massive U.S. investments there, hardly bids well for the continent's relations with the United States. As for East and Southeast Asia, I would be less pessimistic, assuming that we do not unilaterally withdraw from Vietnam; nor do I share what he rightly condemns as the supercilious, semi-racist views of Galbraith and Lippmann. Yet surely Japan is the key country in the area, and Australia the next one, with which we should concern ourselves. Our maintenance of our alliance with Tokyo, as with Canberra, is much more important than the other states in that part of the world. In short, regionalism sounds good, we should pursue it in general, and in some areas of the world it may turn out well, but I would not want to bet too much money on it.

Western Europe does seem to me to be a different case. Here the tumbling down of De Gaulle bids fair to give some new impetus to the movement toward European unity. Yet even so there are some caveats. In the first place, European unity has always had two objectives: to increase Europe's power and prosperity while submerging the German question, and to end Europe's vulnerability to the Soviet Union and also, let us note, its dependence upon the United States. I point this out not to indicate that European unity on this basis would be hostile to American interests. On the contrary, I agree with Professor Rostow that this united Europe would remain our ally, and a more healthy and reliable one because a stronger one. But to maintain our alliances with Western Europe and Japan, which I regard as the single most important priority for our foreign policy, requires also that we conduct our policies toward the Soviet Union and China with this priority in mind.

Let me, therefore, turn to the Soviet Union. It will have been clear from my paper that I am more pessimistic about Soviet policy in the near future than Professor Rostow is. He seems to feel that there is an almost genuinely secular trend toward improvement of Soviet-American relations. Certainly they are considerably better than they were under Stalin; and in my view, as in his, the mutual determination to avoid nuclear destruction has and will play a key role in limiting our conflict relationship with Moscow. Yet I would repeat that recent trends in Soviet policy indicate a sharp limitation of Soviet desire for détente. The nature of the new technological developments in the arms race, which Professor Rostow did not discuss, seems to me to make agreement in the strategic weapons talks less likely. Nor can I share his hope—or perhaps more accurately his prayer, since I can see little other basis for it—that regionalism in the Middle East as well will eventually bring stability. On the contrary, I should expect the situation there to worsen, although probably not to result in a major Soviet-American confrontation. True, as the four-power negotiations demonstrate, neither Washington nor Moscow wants such a confrontation to ensue; and since neither can control its allies both naturally try to compensate for this. But the scheduled 1971 British withdrawal from the Persian Gulf offers new opportunities for Soviet penetration, and while one must hope that Iran and Saudi Arabia will be able to contain this threat, at least the naval and air power vacuum that will result will cause problems for the United States.

More generally, given the restraints that they and we have with respect to the threat of nuclear war, and even if—which I much doubt will soon occur—the

Soviet Union were to become for all practical purposes de-ideologized, why should we assume that a post-Communist Russia would be any less expansionist than pre-Communist Russia? Indeed, given the Soviet Union's much greater power, why not more so? Why should any strong Russia allow the reunification of Germany? Why should it not expand to its south? And even a post-Communist Russia would hardly have its foreign policy determined by its dissident intellectuals, any more than Russia did in 1890. On the contrary, post-Communist Russia, if it comes, is more likely to be an expansionist military dictatorship than a liberal democracy. Professor Rostow seems to me, in short, to be hoping for a world which never has been and probably never will be—a "stable" world.

As to China, much the same holds: a post-Maoist regime in Peking, we may hope, might be less hostile to us, and, we should hope, just as hostile to Moscow; but it will hardly be either democratic or in favor of stability. Like any strong Chinese government, it will want to expand and will only accept stability if it has to.

In short, then, our relations with our two major enemies, while somewhat easier because they are now so hostile to each other, are still likely to remain primarily ones of conflict. We should favor neither one nor the other, balance between and work for détente with both (which means improving relations with Peking to where they now are with Moscow), and remain strong.

And, most importantly, we should keep in mind that not our relations with Russia and China but relations with our allies should have first priority for our foreign policy. Only with our allies will we remain secure. Without them we would be isolated and surrounded. Professor Rostow's paper, in my view, takes a different view. For example, when he refers to the non-proliferation treaty as "a constitutional arrangement proposed to the world, of the greatest significance for its future political and security structure," he seems to me not only to place too much hope in the treaty but even more to be too little concerned about what have been in my view the largely justified reservations of some of our allies about how it was negotiated. When Mr. William Foster, then head of the U.S. Arms Control and Disarmament Agency, wrote in *Foreign Affairs* in July 1965 that the non-proliferation treaty would mean some "erosion of alliances," he was in my view unwisely accepting unnecessary damages to our security arrangements. To us the N.P.T. has meant a general halt of proliferation of nuclear weapons. For the Soviets it has meant primarily barring West German access to them in any form. I am in favor of the treaty, and I am opposed to national German nuclear weapons; but I think the N.P.T. will only slow down, not prevent proliferation, which, like King Canute's tide, we cannot stop. Moreover, I fear that the kind of reverence which Professor Rostow shows toward the treaty is an indication of what I find to have been wanting in some of Presidents Kennedy's and Johnson's policies toward Moscow and toward Western Europe and Japan; too much concern with the Soviet Union, and taking the latter too much for granted. I hope the new administration will reverse this; and I see at least some signs that it will.

Finally, I come to what is in my view perhaps the greatest difference between Professor Rostow's ideas and my own: with respect to the domestic situation in the United States. I gather that he thinks it to be less serious than I do. Although he avows himself uncertain of how the United States will stand up to the challenge as he sees it, he does not seem to feel as strongly as I do that some rapid and specific steps are necessary in order to prevent our situation in foreign—as well as domestic—policy becoming much worse than it now is.

I already indicated in my paper how serious I think our domestic situation is. I would only repeat that as much as we may, rightly, condemn the neo-fascist tactics of the radical left, just as we did, I hope, the McCarthyism of the 1950s, we should not, and indeed dare not, be blind or indifferent to the distortions and wrongs in our society to which they are a reaction. To repeat what I said in my paper:

> . . . it is a national shame and an international scandal . . . that in the midst of the greatest af-

fluence the world has ever known so many American blacks and poor live in squalor and neglect. . . .

It is surprising that those in this country who really hold, rather than merely mouth, the view that they are their brothers' keepers should demand that more of our affluence be devoted to assuaging this poverty and hunger.

Let me now turn to the second cause, in my view, of our serious domestic situation: the Vietnam war. I begin by repeating that I shared with Professor Rostow what has been called—in the inevitably distorting shorthand of controversy—the "hawkish" view. I continue to think that our national interest was and is involved in Vietnam. I continue to be opposed to unilateral U.S. withdrawal. But we must, in my view, face two facts, to me highly unpalatable ones, and face them squarely: we have *not* won the war, and the American people are no longer prepared to *try* to win it. We have not won it, in my view, primarily because we gave too much priority to military and not sufficient priority to political considerations. (We forgot how right Clemenceau was when he remarked that war is too serious a matter to be left to generals.) But, most seriously of all, we overestimated the willingness of American public opinion to support for years what has come to seem to them to be an open-end struggle.

I deliberately do not deal here with the arguments

of those, clearly not including Professor Rostow, that we should not have fought the war in the first place, or with those like Senator Fulbright who first led the Tonkin Gulf resolution through the Senate and now roam the land preaching neo-isolationism. But it seems to me that I am right in saying that the American people want out of the war, that the new administration is moving more rapidly than the old one to get out of it, that we will get out at best on terms which will probably be seen by most abroad and at home as something much short of victory and by many as a defeat, and that the American people will not soon again be ready to accept either such massive burdens of blood and treasure or the assurances of their elected rulers that such burdens will be brief and rewarding.

When one adds to these two factors the growing feeling here at home against the "military-industrial complex"—and I should think, as President Eisenhower did, that there is some reason for concern, the weariness with high taxes, and the proper concern for our domestic crises, we have indeed grave reasons for concern about the future of American foreign policy.

This policy has been, in my view, overextended in some areas of the world. It has suffered from a kind of neo-Wilsonianism, a conviction that it (a) should and (b) could create peace and stability, if not democracy, throughout the world. Now whether it should seems to me doubtful—after all, we have not done so well in Vietnam. But, as I have indicated above—and this to me seems the clincher—I doubt even more that the American people would be willing for us to try. Thus for reasons of both foreign and domestic policy, reasons which in my view are compelling, we should limit our commitments, as I have said in my paper, to our main allies in the developed world and otherwise to the containment of Russian and Chinese—*not* Communist—expansionism in key strategic areas, as well as to such humanitarian aims as the prevention of hunger and the encouragement of economic development, particularly through technical aid.

It has been the "vital center," the hitherto existing consensus of moderate conservatives and moderate liberals, which has supported until now the kind of foreign policy which Professor Rostow advocates, ever since in 1940 the fall of France convinced them that they could no longer comfortably continue to opt out of the world. The Vietnam war and domestic ferment have split this consensus, or at least seriously weakened it, in favor of extremes on the right and left, neither of whom shares its objectives in foreign policy.

It is more difficult, in my view, to estimate the true meaning and future of domestic discontent, since it is centered not in the majority but in minorities: blacks, poor, and alienated students and youth. It arises from the glaring contrast between affluence and poverty, between democratic and humanitarian ideals and all too often discriminatory and inhumane practices. It interacts strongly with the opposition to the Vietnam war and thereby to priorities in expenditure of men and money for arms and aid abroad.

Yet the backlash against what is seen by much if not most of the white middle and working class as the unjustified demands of these alienated groups, has already all too clearly demonstrated that their demands will not soon be met. On the contrary, the backlash against black ghetto riots and more recently against violent student demonstrations may well for a time—but hardly forever, successfully repress the claims of the alienated in our society. If so, we will live in another and, for me, worse America.

But *whatever* happens will be bad for the kind of continuing global commitment to stability which Professor Rostow seems to advocate, or at least to envisage. For the domestic controversy itself will inevitably, even more than it does now, draw attention and appropriations away from foreign and military policy objectives. Moreover, both the radicals of the left and the radicals of the right are neo-isolationists. They want to withdraw from the world to concentrate on their particular prescriptions for what is wrong with us at home.

Do not misunderstand me. I do not maintain that the center will lose control of U.S. foreign policy. Nor do I believe that either the radical left or the radical right will gain control of it. What I do think likely, however, is that this consensus, in order to maintain its control, will have—indeed increasingly will want—to limit its objectives, along, I suspect, the lines that I have outlined. It will, I think, both have to and want to do this in order to remain a consensus, and in order, by reallocation of resources to pressing domestic problems, to remain a consensus in domestic affairs as well. And it will try to undertake this limitation and reallocation in a coming decade in which, as I have tried to demonstrate, the problems it will face with Moscow and Peking, although in some ways different, will hardly be less dangerous, and may be more so, than in the 1960s.

I thus, in conclusion, revert to the note on which I began. I wish that I could be as optimistic, or even as little pessimistic, as Professor Rostow seems to be. But I cannot. And indeed, I would submit, it is perhaps better, in foreign policy estimates and therefore in prescriptions, to err, if at all, on the side of pessimism. We may make mistakes thereby, but they will probably not be as serious ones as the ones we recently have fallen prey to, and from which we must now try to extricate ourselves. If my pessimistic diagnosis turns out to be wrong, and Professor Rostow's to be right, so much the better. No one will be happier than I. But if mine turns out to be right, our reach will even more have exceeded our grasp than in the last few years—with what consequences I hesitate to predict.

Let us, therefore, with Professor Rostow, hope and

pray for the best; but let us also, prudently and even more prayerfully, prepare for something much less. If the latter comes true, the summer soldiers and sunshine patriots will rush off to both extremes, and those of us who will remain in the vital center will have our hands full to husband our resources, limit our objectives, and ride out the storm.

WALT W. ROSTOW

I

There is so much with which I agree in Professor Griffith's paper that, upon reading it, I rather shared Paul Ward's (Baltimore *Sun*) reaction, who asked: "About what will you debate?"

We both regard détente as a possible but uncertain process; we identify the forces making for détente and obstructing it in quite similar if not identical terms; we both regard the outcome as one to be determined by forces at work throughout the world arena, including forces at work in American society itself; our prescriptions, therefore, touch on the whole sweep of American policy rather than on the narrow terrain of United States-Soviet relations.

To serve the purpose of this exercise, therefore, I propose to heighten in my response certain possible differences of analysis and emphasis. The purpose is not contention or confrontation, as the old saying goes. It is to permit us, on the occasion of this joint meeting, to open up for more detailed examination certain substantial underlying issues which, we both agree, bear on the central question.

My observations will bear in particular on:

—The dynamic process by which we have arrived at the possibility, at least, of détente—in particular, as it bears on the developing regions of Asia, the Middle East, Africa, and Latin America.

—The nuclear question, alliances, and détente.

—Vietnam and Asia.

—The problems of domestic American society and their relation to détente and our foreign policy in general.[1]

II

I agree with Professor Griffith that Soviet and American views of détente are not symmetrical. But the fact that Khrushchev — and other Soviet leaders — view "peaceful coexistence" as the "intensification of the class struggle by all means short of interstate war" does not, in itself, determine what real possibilities are, in fact, open to Moscow in the evolving international environment. Professor Griffith argues correctly that an atmosphere of détente gives greater scope to an independent stance by the small powers. But this kind of assertiveness has pre-détente, independent roots. Smaller nations have been maneuvering for a more independent role on the world scene for many years—even at the height of cold war confrontation. Their relative success in standing up straight (as opposed to "leaning to one side") is one of the conditions which has led Moscow in the direction of détente.

After all, the first of the nations to assert itself against bi-polarity and to stand up straight was Yugoslavia. It did so in 1948 at the most intense period of the cold war. The impulse among the weaker states of the world to exploit the cold war competition to find an area of independence goes far back into the late 1940s and early 1950s. It was, evidently, accelerated after the Cuba missile crisis and a reduction in fear of the Soviet Union.

As it has progressed and begun to take shape in the form of regional arrangements, it has diminished the possibilities of Soviet and, also, of United States intrusion and influence.

There is, in fact, something a little old-fashioned about Professor Griffith's use of the phrase "third world." Both the United States and its adversaries tended to think as late as the early 1960s of Asia, the Middle East, Africa, and Latin America as "the underdeveloped areas"; while various efforts were made to align them as a bloc to put pressure on the richer northern half of the globe. In a quiet way—notably, since the failure of the Algerian conference in 1965—we have seen a quite remarkable change in these parts of the world as they have come to realize that their primary tasks of association lie within their regions rather than in some transcendent poor man's club. It is an incomplete trend—a direction of movement, not a completed process. But it deserves to be noted.

I sense throughout Professor Griffith's analysis a view of these regions which would regard them, in my judgment excessively, as evolving in reflex to United States-Soviet relations. I would regard them somewhat more as caught up in authentic revolutions of their own, in which they seek to find a place of strength and dignity in the world through association with each other, while not denying the reality of their interdependencies with the United States and other major powers.

Perhaps this difference in emphasis accounts for the fact that Professor Griffith's periodization of the cold war, as opposed to mine, does not include Khrushchev's post-Sputnik thrust into the developing world and his setback.

So far as substance is concerned, I would rate as a factor making for détente the rising nationalist assertiveness of the developing continents and their movement towards regionalism. Moreover, while in no way underestimating the vicissitudes which they face and will face in the generation ahead, I regard his dictum about their future as too pat and, depending on what we and others do by way of assistance, too pessimistic: "Above all, the third world will become less democratic, more disorderly, more intractable, and more hungry." This we can argue on the spot if our listeners do not regard it as diversionary.

But to put my central point succinctly, whatever Khrushchev may have hoped about the possibilities of

"intensification of a class struggle" in the developing
world—and I believe he hoped a great deal—Soviet
disabuse with the possibilities in those regions is a major
factor in tipping an inherently chancy equation toward
détente.

III

Now a word about nuclear weapons and alliances.

Again, I think the attractive phrase, "atomic weapons
make bad alliances," is too pat. The American nuclear
capacity is the ultimate base for our alliances in Europe,
Asia, and, in the end, in Latin America. When one has
lived through the major confrontations of the 1960s,
it is borne in that, at critical moments, the non-Communist world looks with unambiguous reliance to the
United States, whatever previous diplomatic postures
and political rhetoric have been.

This was so during the Berlin confrontation of 1961-
62; the OAS became, indeed, a band of brothers during
the Cuba missile crisis; a great deal of Indian rhetoric
was quickly stripped away when they confronted the
Chinese at their frontiers in 1962, and, with Moscow
uncertain, it was to Washington that New Delhi looked.
And all of non-Communist Asia, in fact, looks over its
shoulder at the United States every time a nuclear
weapon is detonated on the Chinese mainland.

If Professor Griffith was referring to the same point
that I made in my paper; namely, that an independent

national nuclear capability, with an asserted sovereign right to fire, tends to dilute alliances, then I would agree his dictum holds for Moscow as well as for Washington.

It is against this background that I believe Professor Griffith's analysis of the interests involved in a non-proliferation treaty for both Moscow and Washington are incomplete. There is more to it for Moscow than "preventing West Germany from maintaining a thermonuclear capability." They are concerned—as we are—with the wild cards in the deck that would be introduced into international diplomacy if, say, Israel, Japan, and India were to become nuclear powers. How would they handle Arab pressures for access to nuclear weapons in the first case? What might China do in the second? What would happen to the Pakistani-Chinese relationship in the third, including the possibility of a Pak request for access to Chinese nuclear weapons?

I confess, also, to a certain sympathy with the intervention in the question and answer period of May 8 by the Counsellor of the British Embassy. There is behind the non-proliferation treaty and the thrust towards détente more than *realpolitik*. There is a simple human perception that nuclear weapons are a sword of Damocles hanging over the human race and anything that limits the possibilities of their employment without shifting the relative balance of Communist-non-Communist power is intrinsically a good thing.

In the end, it is this human perception which gives

us a chance of getting the non-proliferation treaty through the parliaments of the world, despite the nationalist resentments and anxieties it inherently stirs.

IV

In reading Professor Griffith's passages on Vietnam and Asia, I found a number of points to mark. How substantial our differences are in fact, I could not detect. But, perhaps now we shall find out.

We might begin with his observation: "If Washington pulls out unilaterally and Hanoi thus wins, Moscow could well thereby be encouraged to indulge in further aid to national liberation struggles. (This would be even more true of Peking.)" This certainly could be one substantial consequence of an American withdrawal from South Vietnam.

But United States forces were not put into Vietnam —nor was the SEATO treaty passed in the Senate— merely to frustrate the technique of guerrilla warfare conducted across international frontiers. It has been a ruling judgment of American policy since the Japanese moved into Indochina in 1941 that Southeast Asia (including the Burmese flank of the Indian subcontinent) is an area of major direct security interest to the United States. The consequences of abandoning that position— which are involved in a withdrawal of United States forces from South Vietnam—are fundamental to the United States position on the world scene. After acting on our commitment, as we have acted, and then with-drawing, no one in Asia would be likely to trust his ties to the United States. I would guess that Indian and Japanese policy towards nuclear weapons would promptly shift. I would guess that there would be a most intense, bitter and disruptive debate in the United States, leading to a weakening of our commitments in Europe and in the Middle East as well as in Asia. Both Professor Griffith's analysis and mine suggest that the Soviet Union and China, under such circumstances, could not restrain themselves from moving in one way or another—and not necessarily through "national lib-eration struggles" alone—to exploit this phase of domes-tic disarray in the United States and a shaking of the alliance structure built since the 1940s.

Then, I suspect, as the reality of the threat to the balance of power in Asia and in Europe became clear, we would see the United States returning to the world scene rather convulsively, after the Russians and Chinese had made their commitments to exploit the openings we had created.

It is the possibility of something like this sequence which led me, at the close of my paper, to bring into focus what I called the game of American roulette we have played in the world arena since 1916.

President Johnson alone can speak for himself; but it may have been something like this sequence that he had in mind in the following passage from his talk at

San Antonio on September 29, 1967:

I cannot tell you tonight as your President—
with certainty—that a Communist conquest of
South Vietnam would be followed by a Communist
conquest of Southeast Asia. But I do know there
are North Vietnamese troops in Laos. I do know
that there are North Vietnamese trained guerrillas
tonight in northeast Thailand. I do know that
there are Communist-supported guerrilla forces
operating in Burma. And a Communist coup was
barely averted in Indonesia, the fifth largest nation
in the world.

So your American President cannot tell you—
with certainty—that a Southeast Asia dominated
by Communist power would bring a third world
war much closer to terrible reality. One could
hope that this would not be so.

But all that we have learned in this tragic century strongly suggests to me that it would be so.
As President of the United States, I am not prepared to gamble on the chance that it is not so.
I am not prepared to risk the security—indeed, the
survival—of this American Nation on mere hope
and wishful thinking. I am convinced that by seeing this struggle through now, we are greatly
reducing the chances of a much larger war—perhaps a nuclear war. I would rather stand in Viet-

nam, in our time, and by meeting this danger now, and facing up to it, thereby reduce the danger for our children and for our grandchildren.

It is in this somber setting—which, I can attest, was the setting in which President Kennedy viewed the problem of Laos and Vietnam—that the costs and burdens, alternatives and gambits in that area must be viewed.

The evidence is very strong that that is, in fact, the way the governments in Asia judge the matter in private councils—from Djakarta to Seoul, from New Delhi, Singapore, and Rangoon to Tokyo—whatever their public formulations or silences may be.

It is true that the strains on the United States of the Vietnam effort have been great. And it is almost certainly true that, for stability in Asia over the long run, the Asians themselves will have to do more, if the American commitments there are to remain viable. As I tried to emphasize in my initial paper, many Asians have come to understand this. But any serious discussion of Vietnam must begin with the assessment of the real alternatives and the stakes at issue made by two Presidents who had every conceivable interest in emerging with a less somber assessment and softer options.

I know well the range of arguments that suggest that United States withdrawal might not have the consequences they perceived. But, as Secretary Rusk often used to say, "A citizen—even a Secretary of State—can go back to a President and say: 'Sorry, sir, my hopeful assessment was wrong.'" A President must live with the decisions that he makes—and so must the nation.

In this setting I have a few minor points to make.

First: "The United States never fought the Vietnam war with full priority for political and social modernization, a policy without which no guerrilla war can be won." In the first place, this is not an historically true statement; for example, the case of Greece, or even Malaya. I don't know what "full priority" means; but it is a simple fact that very considerable political, social, and economic modernization has taken place in South Vietnam over recent years. It can be seen in the statistics of agricultural and industrial production, as well as in education and the unique effort to build a constitutional system via free elections at a time of war.

Second, since Hanoi decided to introduce regular North Vietnamese units in the course of 1964, the war in Vietnam has not been wholly a guerrilla war. Most of the Communist fighting men now are not guerrillas, but regular soldiers. Many of the engagements outside the Delta have been between substantial regular units, not guerrilla forces. For the past three and a half years, the war could be better described (in I, II, and III Corps) as a conventional war without a fixed front. It has also been a war in which, progressively, the Viet Cong have been superseded by North Vietnamese regulars, even in Viet Cong main force units.

I would also make two observations on Professor Griffith's comments on Japan. On balance, the Japanese want détente; but they are passionately concerned that Formosa not be turned over to the Chinese Communists. And it is this issue which is the ultimate source of the rigidity Professor Griffith deplores in United States policy towards mainland China. In all the other dimensions of our approach to mainland China, substantial and recurrent efforts have been made to start a process of normalization. But with Peking, also, the fate of Formosa appears to be central.

Equally, I do not believe United States relations with Japan can be seriously discussed without reference not merely to Okinawa but also to what responsibilities Japan is prepared to undertake on behalf of stability and progress in Asia, including a role in helping monitor the frontiers in a new Southeast Asia settlement.

Now a minor point, but potentially interesting if true. Professor Griffith regards North Vietnam as one of the countries most dedicated to obstructing détente. This may well be true now; but it may not be true once peace is achieved in Southeast Asia. Hanoi may well have an interest in good United States-Soviet relations as a protection against what is, in the long pull, inevitably the North Vietnamese security problem; that is, its independence vis-à-vis China. Harbingers of this perspective can already be seen, among other points, in

the capitals where Hanoi's economic emissaries have
been exploring the possibilities of postwar economic
assistance — mainly capitals in the non-Communist
world.

Taken all together, I find it difficult to understand
the object of Professor Griffith's instruction to us. To
whom would he apply the judgment that we have been
engaged in a "neo-Wilsonian attempt to make over
the world in our own image of peace and stability"?
When has our policy been based on a "reach and universal stability" beyond our grasp?

As I understand United States policy in the postwar
years, it has been based on an attempt to maintain the
balance of power in Europe and in Asia; to prevent the
intrusion of major extra-continental military power
into the Western Hemisphere; and on that basis, to
seek the conditions for stable peace with our adversaries
through negotiation.

The problem of Vietnam involved the judgment of
those who bore constitutional responsibility that the
balance of power in Asia was involved and it must be
held. This, presumably, is a principle which Professor
Griffith would support.

Beyond these critical sensitive areas, the United States
government has gone about its business, trying to keep
out of as many of the world's inevitable crises as it
could. It fully assumed that this was a world inherently
volatile which would, increasingly, have to manage its

own affairs. As I tried to emphasize in my paper for these sessions, that is one of the reasons that we have thrown our weight behind regionalism.

It is true the United States has done all it could think of to do in building the institutions for stable peace and to move our relations with Moscow towards normalcy; but that, presumably, is not Professor Griffith's point.

I have been in and out of the government since August 1945. I have never known a time when the net interest and bias of a President was not to keep out of an international problem, if there was any way of doing so compatible with his oath of office and his view of the nation's abiding interests. And no decision is taken more reluctantly than the decision to commit United States military force.

V

It is worth underlining these possible differences of view about Vietnam and Asia because they bear on the view to be taken of the strains imposed by the war in Vietnam on our domestic society.

If there was or there is a soft option which would have permitted the balance of power in Asia to be held by some easier course, no one has put it forward inside or outside the government. I can attest that all published and spoken proposals were attentively and, even, eagerly explored. But if the loss of the balance of power in Asia is involved, then the burdens that we have carried at home have to be faced—on Professor Griffith's analysis as well as on mine.

I have been greatly struck, in many extended discussions with opponents of our policy in Vietnam, that when all the debating is done, if they are candid, they say: "Let us pull out of Asia. I don't care what happens in Asia." That is a lucid argument which I respect but with which I disagree. Once it is agreed that we have abiding vital interests in the place where two-thirds of humanity live, then the stakes become such that a good deal of pain can be borne.

The nature of the pain—aside from casualties taken in the field—should also be examined.

With all due respect for members of the New Left, with some of whom I now cheerfully live and work, I find it difficult to impute to them the idea that this is a period in our history when we must turn to improve the quality of our society. As Professor Griffith may recall, it was exactly that theme which suffused a good deal of the work on American society which we did at the Center for International Studies at M.I.T. in the years 1955-58. The phrase "The New Frontier," for example, arose explicitly from a vision which looked beyond the age of the automobile and television to the tasks and challenges of improving the quality of the round of life in modern times.

And, of course, our work at M.I.T. was part of a

much larger stream, yielding such substantial efforts as the Rockefeller Brothers Fund Panel Reports and the Report of the President's Commission on National Goals, entitled *Goals for Americans,* published in 1960.

So far as legislation can play a part in improving the quality of life and solving the problem of "American blacks and poor" living "in squalor and neglect," the 1960s have seen the greatest legislative effort of the century in President Johnson's Great Society program.

I make this point not for trivial debating purposes but for a more substantial reason. I do not believe that the war in Vietnam is the reason why Congress has not voted more funds to carry forward these programs. In a way, I wish it were so; because, when the war is ended, I could be confident that large additional resources would flow to these purposes. The resources are evidently there. In a nation with a GNP of $900 billion, with military allocations at 10 percent of GNP, or less, and GNP growing at 4 percent or better (therefore, with an increment each year to allocate among private and public purposes of $35-$40 billion), we have the resources. But the will to use them has diminished. What we have seen in our country is a conservative reaction against such allocations, primarily triggered by the methods of advocacy used by more radical Negroes and whites. The law and order reaction has brought with it restraints on spending for just the purposes Professor Griffith and I would support.

This is a matter on which none of us can afford to be fuzzy. If we are to get on with the job, we shall have to rebuild the political foundations in this country for such an effort. And that is a real piece of business. It is gravely obstructed by the cult of confrontation.

I would also note that it is no new objective to seek "a higher, more humane quality in our daily lives than the needless rush of technology offers." The problems posed by men having to find their private destiny and expression for their talents in a highly structured bureaucratic environment is, after all, the central theme in a great many novels written since 1945 and in a good deal of professional social analysis. With no great claim to originality, I was able to define "Bureaucracy, Innovation and the Individual" as one of the key problems on the American agenda when I put *The United States and the World Arena* to bed in 1958.

The real issue is: What do we do about it? What concrete kinds of organizational structures and innovations in government, business, the universities, and elsewhere will actually give the individual greater scope and responsibility and a greater sense of shaping his own destiny? There are things that have been done about it. And there are things to do about it. But it will take hard, practical work in many settings to reshape our institutions in this wholesome direction. And those efforts are not likely to be advanced merely by shouting about the problem.

Now a brief word on the military-industrial complex. I know tolerably well the story of the United States military budget since 1945—including President Truman's pre-June 1950 view that $15 billion should be its absolute ceiling and President Eisenhower's obsession with the Great Equation, arrived at on the cruiser *Helena* before he came to office. I have seen something of the budgetary process directly as it bore on allocations to military purposes since 1961. It is true the Joint Chiefs of Staff argue for more rather than less, as it is almost their constitutional duty to do. It is true certain business firms are interested in more rather than less. But it is also true that the net bias in American political life—as it comes through to the President from the Congress and as it bears on the President himself—is to constrain, not to expand, the military budget. Elected officials in our system are under great simultaneous pressure to allocate more tax money for civil purposes and to cut taxes. This dual pressure far outweighs normal political pressure for increased military outlays which are based, in the end, on a reluctantly arrived at judgment as to what reasonable security for the nation requires.

Again, this does not mean there are not advocates for more. It does not mean military requirements should not be scrutinized and debated. It does mean we must be careful to put the notion of "a military-industrial complex" into the full context of American political life with all its lively countervailing pressures.

But, in the end, I am wholly in agreement with Professor Griffith that there is a sensitive interplay between our problems at home—and how we deal with them—and what we can do abroad. The art of policy is to move forward at home while patiently, brick by brick, building the structure of what may in time prove to be a stable peace.

But along this way there can be only peril for the nation—including peril to the quality of our society—if we revert to the dangerous game of American roulette.

DISCUSSION

FIRST SESSION

BENJAMIN F. SCHEMMER, President and Publisher, *Journal of the Armed Forces:* If we accept your proposal to limit ABM (anti-ballistic missile) deployment to the extent that we do not press for ABMs to defend cities, on what basis, if any, can we justify continued expenditures for damage-limiting, for AWACS (Airborne Warning and Control System), F-106-X, advanced manned interceptor, Nike Hercules, Continental Air Defense, Hawk sites in the U.S.? Put differently, if we accept the conclusion I believe you stated, why don't we pay for Safeguard to protect our assured destruction capability by phasing out our damage-limiting program?

DR. GRIFFITH: I don't know all of the technical details involved but my impression is that Safeguard, the present proposal, as compared to the Sentinel proposal of the Johnson Administration, moves quite strongly in this direction in the sense that there would be protection to missile sites by Safeguard but that there would not be the expenditures on damage-limiting capability which were planned with Sentinel. I think the fundamental argument for this relates to cost effectiveness: the damage-limiting capability of the Sentinel system, for example, as compared to what one could anticipate that the Soviet Union would produce in increased offensive capability to degrade or overcome it.

As you may know, there is an extreme difference of scientific and technical opinion on this subject and there are plenty of statistics available for both sides. Even if I were a scientist, which I am not, I'm not sure that I would myself be confident of my own opinion on the subject.

It seems to me that a more effective case can be made for protection of missile sites, given the technological situation with which we are now confronted than for a (cost-effectivewise) useful deployment around cities.

There is one final point I should add, though, and that relates to the Soviet ABM deployment which, as our reports indicate, has been primarily around Moscow and which appears to have been suspended for some time. It's unclear, of course, why it was suspended but it's at least a logical assumption that this was intended to improve its technological effectiveness.

ROBERT R. LOCKLIN, Administrative Assistant to Senator John Sparkman: You stated in your paper that deployment of ABM was a destabilizing influence because Soviet intelligence efforts were able only to judge the quantitative and not the qualitative aspects of the ABM. Does not this ignore intelligence efforts by the Soviet Union other than overflights? I wonder whether or not the deployment of ABM is really as destabilizing as one might otherwise conclude.

DR. GRIFFITH: I didn't say or at least I think I didn't say that ABM was by definition destabilizing. It seems to me that MIRV (Multiple Independently-Targeted Re-entry Vehicle) can be considered a destabilizing weapon in terms of the enormous leap forward in the destructive capability and in terms of the near-impossibility of inspection.

I said that ABM could be either stabilizing or destabilizing. At the present time I would regard it as stabilizing in terms of protection of missile sites, of assured destruction capability, and quite possibly destabilizing, depending on one's cost-effectiveness arguments, with respect to deployment around cities.

But I agree with you that the Soviet Union, almost by definition, would have greater potentiality to determine effectiveness of ABM or MIRV in this country, which is a more open society, than we would have in the Soviet Union. This has been the case, of course, with every weapon up to now. I would assume, with the much greater difficulty of verification by satellite photography, that the Soviet Union, and quite possibly the United States as well, would set up other means to try to achieve some kind of verification. Given the asymmetry of the two societies, it seems to me likely that the Soviet Union would have a better chance of this than we would.

JOHN L. CALDWELL, Chamber of Commerce of the United States: In your enumeration of factors favoring East-West détente, I don't believe that you made any reference to the role of trade that was being spurred by this détente. What role do you see for trade in future East-West relations? Do you, for example, favor the granting of most-favored-nation treatment on a selective basis to East European countries?

DR. GRIFFITH: That's a very valid criticism of my presentation. I should have mentioned something about trade. I don't think that up to now it has been a major factor in East-West détente because it has been quantitatively relatively small, compared to West European trade, but I think it could be. Indeed, I would argue that one of the major potentialities, perhaps even *the* major potentiality, that the United States has for constructive influence in Eastern Europe is in the field of East-West trade. Our failure to use trade has simply meant that it has been used by the Germans, French, Italians, or British. We have tended, out of what I regard as counterproductive ideological hostility or pro-

tectionist sentiments or the combination of both—
Polish hams, for example—to limit uselessly and ineffec-
tively our own possibilities.

If the United States were capable of enforcing something like an international trade embargo toward certain Communist countries, one could certainly argue,
with respect to Eastern Europe and the Soviet Union,
that this might make some sense. I would argue that
it would for some and not for others but that isn't the
real question.

The point is that we are not capable of doing so with
respect to the main Western European countries and
Japan.

I also think that past American administrations—
I can't really say yet about the new administration because it's too early—have been politically undiscrimi-
nating in their use of such things as the most-favored-
nation treatment. It, for example, does not exist for
Rumania but does exist for Poland. I can see no political or other justification for this situation. It seems
to me that the one thing which logically should be done
would be to grant most-favored-nation treatment to
Rumania. I think there is a serious question whether it
should be continued with respect to Poland.

With respect to Yugoslavia, I think that we have
tended unnecessarily to limit our potentialities there,
particularly with respect to tourism. We have not

pushed as rapidly as I think we could to try to reach agreement with the Yugoslav government toward the use of blocked dinars for joint American-Yugoslav investments in such things as tourist hotels, for example. There are more than a million Germans who go every year to the Dalmatian coast, one of the major sources of Yugoslav revenue. A lot of Americans do too. I don't see why United States enterprise should not be more involved in this.

I think that East-West trade can rarely be used now, except for an embargo on a very restricted list of genuinely strategic goods, as an effective, direct political weapon. But it can be used for the pursuit of détente and, incidentally, for the profit of American business. I think it's unfortunate that it has not been used sufficiently up to now.

There are, as you probably know, hearings going on in a Senate committee on this subject and I would hope that they would result, with administration support, if that is forthcoming—I wish it would be—in rationalizing and improving our posture on East-West trade.

JAMES D. CARY, Copley News Service: In your presentation you said that deployment of MIRV could move the United States toward the most destabilizing posture of all, a potential first-strike capability. If you are going to have more warheads or multiple warheads on a missile, are you not going to reduce the megatonnage of each one of these warheads and, therefore, lessen rather than increase the ability to knock out underground sites? Aren't you going to lessen your ability to destroy their strategic-missile installations although you may increase your ability to destroy their above-ground installations? How could this be a first-strike capability?

DR. GRIFFITH: I said that it could be interpreted as a move toward a first-strike capability, if one were to exclude the probable Soviet response, which presumably would be a sufficient increase in Soviet hardening of sites and Soviet offensive capability so that this would not occur.

But as I understand, the point with MIRV, with respect to its use for counterforce capability against hardened or superhardened sites, is not the number of warheads and not the size of the warhead, it is the accuracy of the targeting mechanism. The accuracy of MIRV is a matter of public knowledge. There is a statistical table on it in testimony by the then Under Secretary of Defense (Paul) Nitze before one of the congressional committees in terms of its assured destruction capability, including of hardened sites. The accuracy of MIRV is so much greater than the Minuteman or Polaris that in fact it is a much more effective counterforce weapon than a much larger warhead with much less accuracy. The so-called CEP (circular error of probability) with respect to MIRV is very much less.

CHARLES MOELLER, Metropolitan Life Insurance Company: You dealt very thoroughly with the bars to détente, the East-West Europe split, China-Russia, North and South Vietnam, North and South Korea, East-West Germany, the arms race. You mentioned as one of the most important factors for the 1970s the Middle East situation, the Arabs and the Israelis. Would you please further explain its importance as a bar to détente?

DR. GRIFFITH: There are two reasons, it seems to me, why it is potentially a serious bar to détente. First, the possibility of the United States' controlling its allies and the Soviet Union's controlling its allies, in terms of limiting the prospects of another Israeli-Arab war, is quite small as compared, for example, to the situation in Europe. Second, there is the area of arms shipment, in which we should make our most serious attempt to contain the possibility of another war. The fundamental destabilizing factor, in addition to the territorial and other disputes, has been the enormous input of arms into the area. This began to be intensified from the Soviet side almost immediately after the 1955 Geneva Summit Conference, when Khrushchev sent one of his then associates, Shepilov, to Cairo and shortly thereafter Czechoslovak arms shipments to Cairo began. Indeed, the major weapon of the Soviet Union in extending its influence in the third world has been arms shipments: Guatemala, Cuba, the Middle East, Vietnam, Black Africa, wherever you wish. One of the most serious problems we face is how to bring about at least a decline in arms shipment.

As to the prospect of actual settlement of one or more of the major issues between the Israelis and the Arabs, I am very pessimistic. It seems to me that it's very unlikely that a settlement will occur very soon. The very lack of settlement, the rising frustrations of the Arabs over the lack of settlement, the continued input of arms into the area, the determination of the Israelis to maintain substantially their present territorial boundaries, all of these seem to me to make it more likely that there will be, not a major Soviet-American confrontation, but some kind of renewed hostility. It may be that we will never be quite sure when these border conflicts become in fact hostilities. I don't know that I would agree with the UN Secretary General that in fact war has already broken out, but certainly the level of border hostilities is rising rapidly.

The latest Israeli retaliatory raid on the Nile is an indication of how far this can go. Russian prestige is greatly engaged. The number of Russian military technicians, pilots, and so on, in the UAR and in Syria has increased very greatly. The possibility of a serious Soviet-American crisis developing is certainly there.

As in the case of the escalation of the arms race, so in the case of the rising tension in the Middle East, this also tends to have a countereffect. Both Washington and Moscow try negotiation to prevent a confrontation.

The final point, which I think I may have mentioned briefly in my initial remarks, is that the present crisis in the Middle East, which relates essentially to Israel, Jordan, Syria, and the UAR, will probably be augmented in the early 1970s by the power vacuum which is likely to develop in the Persian Gulf area with the withdrawal of the British. Unlike the other areas I have mentioned, this will involve major oil-producing areas which Nasser has long been anxious to control, areas in which the Russians also are very interested. It will involve the attempts—individually or collectively —of Iran and Saudi Arabia to try to prevent the area from falling under some foreign control.

The stake here, in terms of the amount of oil involved in Kuwait alone, for example, is so great that I think that the prospects of a rise in tension are quite serious.

CLIVE M. ROSE, Counselor, British Embassy: I would like to take issue with you, if I may for a moment, on your remarks on the reasons why Britain favors détente. You gave four reasons for this. The first one, which you expect me to take issue with, I'm sure, is that Britain is militarily weak. Of course it is true that Britain has decided to withdraw from the Far East and the Persian Gulf, east of Suez, as we call it. This may be regarded by some as a sign of military weakness. In fact it is a sign of sensible use of resources.

The fact that we stayed there too long produced in some people's eyes, a rather absurd situation. Our withdrawal was a sign that we had decided to use our resources in the best way possible and to cut our coat according to our cloth.

This enabled us to make a much fuller contribution to the defense of Europe.

So, far from being militarily weak—and I do want to make this point because I think it is important that your remarks should not go unchallenged—in fact, Britain spends more, a larger percentage of her GNP on defense than any other European NATO country except Portugal.

In fact, we have the largest all-professional army in NATO. We have the largest European navy in NATO and the largest European air force in NATO. So much for the question of British military weakness.

As I say, you gave three other reasons for Britain's favoring a détente. One was, you said, fear of Russia. This is surprising to me. If you really look at it, if you analyze the situation in Europe over the last 20 years, you will see that fear of Russia was what caused us all to get together and form NATO. It is this fear of

Russia which has kept NATO together for this nearly 20 years. Now, it seems to me that, in many ways, fear of Russia is hardly likely to be the thing which would cause Britain to favor a détente. It's fear of Russia which causes Britain to maintain the military strength of the alliance and the military posture which we all agreed to maintain.

If fear of Russia was one of our prime motivations, I would have thought that a détente would rather have the opposite effect. The thing that may happen as the result of a détente, and we have so recognized this in Europe, is a decline of American interest and commitment to Europe. This is something that we are all conscious of.

If this is the thing that might result, then it is hardly likely that we would favor a détente from fear of Russia.

The reasons why we favor détente are basically the same reasons why the United States favors a détente. One of them is that we believe confrontation and tension is dangerous and because of its danger it is necessary constantly to try to work to reduce it. If one doesn't work for a détente then one stands on the status quo and one builds up friction and confrontation and tension, without doing anything to try to remove this source of central conflict. The other reason is that, if one doesn't work for détente, if one sticks on confrontation with military buildups on both sides, then one will have an increasing diversion of resources to military expenditure, which might be better spent on other things such as social problems.

You have the same problems as we do and these are basically the reasons why we favor détente.

Now, sir, I will ask you a question. I think you expressed some doubt about prospects for Western European unity. I think I would call you perhaps a cautious pessimist on Western European unity. Perhaps I am wrong and, if so, I hope you will tell me so. I'm not, of course, a pessimist myself. I'm rather more than a cautious optimist. I believe that enormous progress on European unity has been made in a really very short time, when you take the long span of history, and I believe much more progress will be made in the next five or ten years.

What role would you think a stronger united Western Europe could play in the East-West détente? How can a stronger Western Europe contribute toward the idea of a détente?

DR. GRIFFITH: I'm grateful for the clarification of British policy and I think that your definition of it is probably more precise than some of the definitions which I made. I did not mean when I said that Britain was militarily weak, to mean anything more than in comparison with Japan or France or Germany. It seems to me quite natural that a country which does not regard itself alone or even necessarily with allies as capable of preventing unacceptable damage should be in favor of limiting the risk of nuclear war. This is, of course, true of the United States and it seems to me even more true of Great Britain. I don't think that this is peculiar in any sense to the British Isles.

With respect to what I said about fear of Russia, probably this could be more accurately put as a fear of nuclear war, as you yourself have said.

With respect to the question of European unity, perhaps I should have said that I'm somewhat pessimistic about any prospects in the near future for rapid European political unification. I think there probably will be, after the passing of General de Gaulle, some further progress with respect to economic and perhaps even political unity—and I should hope that this would include the admission of the United Kingdom to the Common Market. But this is not really what I mean by my reference to political unification. Indeed, it seems to me at the present time, with the passing of De Gaulle and with the developing monetary crisis, that the major problem for many of the West European states may become their fear lest West Germany become the predominant power in the Common Market. This may result in some Franco-German rapprochement.

It has often been said that Western European unity may result from a commonly shared fear that particularly frontier industries in Europe may be bought up by American corporations. Western Europe would attempt to overcome the technological gap. There is very much logic in this, but up to now it doesn't seem to have happened. Indeed, European corporations appear still to prefer dealing directly with American corporations rather than uniting with each other.

There is one final point that I should make with respect to the prospects of a strongly united Western Europe playing a role in détente. The most difficult thing to envisage is how you bring about some kind of reunification in the strategic sphere, remembering that Britain and France have nuclear deterrents but Germany does not, while there persists the quite understandable Russian fear of any German access to nuclear weapons.

The general thrust of American policy since the war, favoring a strong and united Europe, continues in my view to be entirely justified. In fact, a strong and united Europe would take a course toward détente stronger, if anything, than that of the United States. A united Europe would probably remain essentially allied with the United States, making it more likely that the Soviet Union would be unable to become predominant either in the strategic weapons field or in the Middle East or elsewhere. After all, the material interests of Western Europe are more clearly involved with the Middle East than those of the United States.

European unification would probably be a very major contribution to prevention of Soviet adventurism. The Soviet Union is clearly interested in dividing Europe rather than having it united.

I wish that I could believe that there will be decisive progress toward European political unification in the next five or ten years. I would be very much in favor of it. I think it's very much in the American interest. I remain somewhat pessimistic about it but I only hope that my predictions will be proven wrong.

MR. SCHEMMER: Professor Griffith, you stated that the Soviets have been deploying some 1,200 of the large-yield but not-too-accurate missile, the SS-9, by now. I have the impression that the President of the United States tonight would have a heart attack if the CIA told him that the Soviets in fact had deployed the 1,200 SS-9s. Since this number differs I think by a factor of 2, 3, or 5 from those cited by Secretary Laird or Deputy Defense Secretary Packard in their recent testimony, what is the source of the number you say?

DR. GRIFFITH: I think the figure I gave of 1,200 includes the SS-9 but also includes other missiles besides the SS-9. It is the total of Soviet land-based ICBMs.

MR. SCHEMMER: Thank you, I'm relieved.

DR. GRIFFITH: But an increasing percentage of those are SS-9s. Altogether the Soviet Union now has a substantially higher number of land-based ICBMs than the United States. The deployment of SS-9s has been very rapid. I think one of the questions which is most difficult to answer, and which will have the greatest influence, probably, not only on the arms race but on Soviet-American relations, is the extent to which the Soviet Union will continue to deploy SS-9s. The significance of this will be even more difficult to gauge if that American MIRV deployment actually occurs. Measuring the relationships strategically between the United States and the Soviet Union in terms of quantity of missile launchers will become increasingly meaningless. Quality differences will emerge. Also, as I tried to point out before, the number of warheads on both sides will not accurately reflect the strategic relationship, because the important question will be the quality of the warheads, that is to say their accuracy.

JOSEPH WHELAN, Library of Congress: There has been some talk this evening about the dissolution of British power east of Suez. What would you think United States policy should be in the future with regard to this larger problem? I am speaking specifically, of course, of the Persian Gulf area.

DR. GRIFFITH: I would assume that the best the

United States could hope for would be an agreement between Iran and Saudi Arabia, with other powers such as Kuwait being involved, which would offer as much local stability and local input into this power vacuum as possible. It may well be, it seems to me, that insofar as Iran is active in this the Soviet interest in improving its relations with Iran will be at least a deterrent against Soviet attempts to stir up trouble, directly or more likely indirectly, through Iraq or the UAR. The Soviet Union may be somewhat deterred from stirring up trouble if this would worsen relations between Moscow and Teheran. That's still in the future.

After Vietnam the United States is going to be extremely reluctant, in the Persian Gulf or wherever else, to run the risk of the kind of involvement which has developed in South Vietnam.

Nevertheless, I would suppose the immediate problem that will face the United States will be the question: To what extent may the American naval force in the area, now extremely small, be increased? This, in turn, it seems to me, will be very much influenced by the extent of Soviet naval presence in the area. For the first time, I think, in the history of the Russian Navy, Imperial or Soviet, a significant Russian naval squadron visited Iraq, Basra, and then Mombasa. This squadron, I think, came from Vladivostok. The possibilities of anything like a major Soviet fleet being stationed in the area are still quite small. But, as we know from the history of naval races in this century, this kind of race can develop very rapidly.

Another very great influence on this race would be the Suez Canal, whether or not it will be open, whether the Soviet navy in the Mediterranean will be able to have free passage into the Red Sea and into the Indian Ocean. It doesn't seem to me very likely that this will occur very soon. Indeed one could argue that it is not particularly in the American interest that the Suez Canal be opened.

All these things, it seems to me, are quite unpredictable. I would think that the initial question that will be posed to the United States, though, would be what Iran and Saudi Arabia might wish. This may determine the extent to which we would deem it desirable to increase our American naval forces in the Indian Ocean or to move into the Persian Gulf.

LIVINGSTONE HARTLEY, Atlantic Council: I am wondering if there might not be a new element in this situation following the fall of De Gaulle. We may now see greater solidarity within the Atlantic Alliance. A year and a half ago NATO adopted the Harmel Report; NATO was going to seek détente as well as deterrence, collectively in the alliance. I am just wondering if you don't get a new element there.

DR. GRIFFITH: After the temporary interruption

caused by the invasion of Czechoslovakia, this has occurred. Indeed, I believe there is a forthcoming visit of the Belgian foreign minister to Moscow and I am sure that these things will be pursued.

But, as in the past, so probably in the future, such a proposal, for example, has been, I think, advanced by NATO at the Reykjavik meeting, suggesting mutual troop withdrawals. But this is not very likely to be agreed upon by the Russians. Their more recent military action has hardly been one of military withdrawal; it rather has been one of military advance.

Indeed, I think that in Czechoslovakia or, for that matter, in East Germany or in Poland, there are adequate political reasons why the Soviet Union would be unlikely now to withdraw troops.

However, I think that this NATO strategy is generally a very sound one, in particular insofar as the Soviets continue to revive their proposal for a European security conference. The intention of the latest proposal is unclear, particularly with respect to the degree to which the United States would be involved. It seems to me that NATO, in general, and the United States, in particular, would be well advised not to take a totally negative attitude toward the proposal, however. On the contrary, an effort should be made to revive the kind of proposals which were made before the invasion of Czechoslovakia involving, for example, mutual troop withdrawals, inspection posts, early warning systems, etc.

JOHANNES F. BUHL, Embassy of Denmark: You mentioned in the statement, sir, that you foresee that the present Soviet leadership may fear certain aspects of détente. The objective of the West is to have a broader détente.

I feel that the military service has come to play an increasing role in Soviet policymaking.

Do you accept this point of view and do you feel that increasing influence of the Soviet military will affect their attitude toward further détente?

DR. GRIFFITH: I think there are signs of increasing Soviet military influence, but I do not share the views of those who maintain that the Soviet military has become or is likely soon to become predominant in the Soviet Union. Such a crisis as Czechoslovakia was last year almost automatically tends to give the Soviet military a quite legitimate opportunity, in the Soviet context, to assert its point of view.

But more importantly, it seems to me, the increasing signs of division within the Soviet leadership mean that in such a divided situation the military will have more influence.

Yet, such things as the canceling of the military parade in Moscow, the speech of [Secretary-General] Brezhnev instead of [Defense Minister] Marshal Grechko at the May Day celebrations and, in general, the appearance of a series of articles in *Kommunist* and elsewhere emphasizing party leadership in the military—these things don't seem to me to indicate that the military is any closer to taking over in the Soviet Union.

I do think, however, that insofar as military influence in the Soviet Union increases, that it is likely to work against a Soviet policy favoring détente. Indeed, this kind of attitude of the military is not confined only to the Soviet Union.

AMBASSADOR LOY W. HENDERSON: I'm Loy Henderson, retired Foreign Service Officer and a member of the faculty at American University at the present.

I must say, before I ask my question, that I am very much impressed by what you say. I agree with nearly everything you say, but there are several points, one point in particular, on which I would like to comment. I feel that you didn't lay enough emphasis on the ideological factor. I know you said that ideology was used as a supporting factor.

During the last 50 years there has hardly been any period of two or three years in which it hasn't been announced that communism was dead in the Soviet Union, that communism no longer was influencing Soviet foreign policy. I can remember, for instance, when the New Economic Policy in the early twenties was announced. Many people, including the press, said: "This means the end of the Communist experiment."

Later, when the Soviet Union joined the League of Nations, people said, "Ah, there is a great change now, they are going to cooperate and work with other nations and they are forgetting their Communist objective." Again, when the Soviet Union formed alliances with France and Czechoslovakia, this was taken as another proof that it was coming out of its shell and willing to work with the non-Communist world.

When Molotov and Hitler signed their pact, a lot of people said, "Well, communism is dead now. How could a Communist state come to an understanding with the Nazis? They really are no longer Communist."

And, a little later, when the Soviet Union announced it was going to reach into east Poland, into the Baltic states and later into Finland, Soviet leaders announced they were not going to socialize anything. Those states could stay like they were, they would be allies, they won't be socialized, the Soviet leaders said. But those states were socialized.

When the Comintern was abolished, again we were in a great euphoria in this country. The papers hailed it as a wonderful thing. That means the end of communism in the Soviet Union, it was said. Yet we saw that even before World War II was over the Soviets were organizing a free Germany, hoping to bring a "free" German government into Germany when the war was over. Already that was the difference in approach after the war. When Stalin died, again there was this same feeling.

It seems to me that we have to bear in mind what is the ultimate aim of the Soviet Union. Is it just for power? Is it for territory? Or is it to build up a machine which, when strong enough, can make moves at various points in the direction of a Communist world? Now, I don't want to exaggerate that. I know that may never be accomplished. I know that, as the years go by, there can be changes in what is meant by a "Communist world."

But don't you feel that we do tend sometimes to just take it for granted that the Soviet state is like any other state, that it doesn't have certain ultimate objectives which sooner or later are going to come in confrontation with us? We can postpone that confrontation—and we should try to postpone it. But shouldn't we bear in mind that there is that innate difference which is still there, that ideological aims are still present in the Soviet Union?

DR. GRIFFITH: If I communicated anything to the contrary, then I communicated badly. I think there is no question that the element of Communist ideology in Soviet foreign policy tends to make it considerably more hostile to the United States and Western Europe than it would be otherwise. I think it would probably be hostile to the United States in any case. The main point I was trying to make about the origins of the cold war was that this hostility would probably have developed even if the Soviet Union had not been Communist. But because it was and is, this intensifies the struggle and is likely to make it continue to be more intensified and longer in duration than it otherwise would be.

I don't believe that the Soviet leadership is a group of cynical Machiavellians who really don't believe in what they profess. I think they do believe in what they profess and will continue to do so.

AMBASSADOR HENDERSON: You mean in communism.

DR. GRIFFITH: In communism, in Marxism—Leninism. I think that increasing numbers of Soviet intellectuals are highly disillusioned with their ideology. The ideology in Eastern Europe, being often identified with Russian imperialism, is even less strong among many of the opposition elements in the population. But this is not true of the Soviet leadership.

There is, I think, no question that the ideological differences between the Communist world and the United States intensify a hostility which would be great in any case.

At the same time, as you pointed out, there have been

serious changes, including, for example, the decline in the credibility of the ideology resulting from the Sino-Soviet split. It is rather difficult to believe in proletarian internationalism when, clearly, communism has become much more national than international. This does not mean that the ideology is dead. I think that perhaps the major intensifying element in the ideology is the way in which it forms the Soviet leaders' picture of the world, a picture which remains fundamentally dichotomic. In their view the capitalist world is hostile to the socialist world, and there can be no such thing as complete détente. The détente must be limited whenever it appears to be bridging this dichotomy.

As I said, when Khrushchev defined peaceful co-existence as the intensification of the class struggle by all means other than interstate war, he meant exactly what he said. He meant that détente would be used and should be used, by the Soviet Union both to limit the risk of nuclear war and to use the decline in tension to intensify the political effort in Western Europe and in Japan. This is one of the dangers of détente, as has been pointed out, with respect, for example, to Western Europe.

My feeling is that up to now it has been perhaps more dangerous to the Soviet Union in Eastern Europe than it has to the United States in Western Europe.

But the problem is that the Soviet Union can much more easily limit its effects in Eastern Europe, by tanks and troops and planes, than the United States can in Western Europe. After all, the equivalent for the Soviet limitation of détente in Czechoslovakia on our part would have been to invade it first.

AMBASSADOR HENDERSON: Don't you think that we are more interested really in détente than the Soviet Union is, in true détente?

DR. GRIFFITH: Oh, there is no question of it. The United States in the Western world tends to view détente as an end in itself.

AMBASSADOR HENDERSON: That's right.

DR. GRIFFITH: The Soviet Union and Communist China tend to view détente as useful in limiting the risk of nuclear war but fundamentally as another means of carrying on the struggle with the West, a struggle which is likely to continue not only for our lifetimes but perhaps beyond that.

CHARLES MAYER, Chairman, Foreign Policy Discussion Group: Sir, I am not entirely sure that détente is really in our best interests. Why would we not be well advised just to wait for any further efforts toward détente until the Soviets and Peking are prepared to make concessions, political concessions.

DR. GRIFFITH: Détente is in our interest primarily because it tends to limit the risk of nuclear war and to limit the risks of a conventional confrontation, for example, in the Middle East. It is also in our interest in this exchange of opportunities and dangers in Western Europe and Eastern Europe—it tends probably to give us more advantages in the long run than the Soviet Union. But I don't see any reason, particularly given the Sino-Soviet hostility, why the United States should make what would amount to unilateral concessions in order to obtain détente. These are neither necessary nor desirable.

In the case of the non-proliferation treaty, this is clearly more in the interests of the Soviet Union than the United States. I think it is in the American interest, although I think that we have caused too much damage to our relations with our allies in our negotiation of it. We have been too anxious to accept what Mr. (William C.) Foster called the erosion of alliances for this. It is in our interest because in general it tends to lower the risk of nuclear war, if the treaty is signed, but this advantage is probably only temporary. The non-proliferation treaty in my view plays the same role that King Canute tried with the tide. It will probably slow down proliferation, but proliferation will occur.

For the Soviet Union the non-proliferation treaty is, in its view, essentially a device to prevent the access of West Germany to nuclear weapons. There is no equivalent danger for us at the present time. Therefore, there is not only no reason for us to make any concessions to get the non-proliferation treaty signed, on the contrary, it is the Soviet Union, since it is more interested in it, which in my view should make the concessions.

In other areas, the advantage or disadvantage may differ. Fundamentally, if the United States plays its cards intelligently, there is no reason why it should have to make more concessions than the Soviet Union. Indeed, with respect to the arms race, as I indicated, the qualitative advantage, in a race which is becoming more qualitative all the while, is on the side of the United States. This does not mean that I think we should pursue it, to try to spend the Soviet Union into bankruptcy —a policy which would be no more successful than the highly mythical Soviet policy of trying to spend us into bankrupcy—which never, I think, really existed. But there is no reason why we should make in this respect unilateral concessions.

STANISLAW PAWLAK, Embassy of the Polish People's Republic: I have some comments on your statement, but I don't like to make them now. Of course I don't agree with many of your opinions, as is obvious, of course.

I would like to know, if you could tell us, please, on what grounds you base your opinion that Poles are rather against than for détente. I would like to draw your attention to some plans which were proposed by our foreign minister in 1957, the so-called Rapacki Plan and then the other plan produced by Mr. Gomulka, the so-called Gomulka Plan.

If you would be so kind to give your opinion of these—I would appreciate it very much.

DR. GRIFFITH: I tried to distinguish and I did not, I suppose, fully enough, between East Germany and Poland with respect to détente. I think that in general the Polish attitude has been considerably more favorable toward détente than that of East Germany.

This does not mean that I endorsed then or endorse now the Rapacki or Gomulka Plans, which in my view, by denuclearizing the American army in Germany, would have worked in favor of the Soviet Union. But I don't think this was the only motive or necessarily the primary motive with respect to these plans.

I was thinking, in respect to Poland, of the invasion of Czechoslovakia. It seems to me that the invasion of Czechoslovakia was a blow against détente and was a part of a more general Soviet move to limit the effects of détente in Eastern Europe.

I think that Mr. (Walter) Ulbricht (East German Communist Party Chief) was probably even more in favor of the invasion of Czechoslovakia than Mr. Gomulka. But Mr. Gomulka supported it also.

And in this specific case it seems to me that whatever the Polish motives may have been, they in fact, "objectively" contributed to a move which was against détente.

It is quite clear that Poland, which is not a divided nation as East Germany is, and which wishes to secure its boundaries—a motive which I would certainly share and support—is in favor of the kind of détente which would tend to move in this direction. But this does not mean that it always supports moves in favor of détente. It seems to me that in the case of the invasion of Czechoslovakia it supported, for whatever motives, a move which was a major blow to détente.

MR. PAWLAK: You are saying a lot about the invasion of Czechoslovakia. Of course we can argue all night about that. I would like to draw your attention only to one fact. If you consider the balance of power in Europe, everybody knows that Europe is divided into blocs. This division is artificial but is a fact. Still, having Czechoslovakia as our neighbor—I don't like to speak of other countries as our neighbor—we have to secure our borders. Czechoslovakia occupies about 1,200 kilometers of very difficult mountain border with Poland. And we have some obligations to Czechoslovakia as a country bound by the same agreement, the Warsaw Pact.

But Czechoslovakia has some obligations to us. We

cannot open our borders unilaterally, even Czechoslovakia knows, if Czechoslovakia goes out of the Warsaw
Pact.

I would like just to make this footnote to what you
are saying.

DR. GRIFFITH: I think this represents the expressed policy of the Polish government. And I would
be convinced that it was in accord with Polish interest
if I thought that Czechoslovakia under Mr. Dubcek
intended to leave the Warsaw Pact. But it clearly did
not. Nor did the Czechoslovak Communist party under
Mr. Dubcek intend to abdicate power. On the contrary, it was determined to keep it.

Unlike Hungary in 1956, which did withdraw from
the Warsaw Pact under the pressure of public opinion,
Czechoslovakia, I think, was determined, for reasons
very similar to those of Poland, to maintain a primary
alliance with the Soviet Union. I think the Soviet
Union invaded Czechoslovakia because it feared the
liberalization going on in that country, which would
not have resulted in parliamentary democracy in my
opinion, either immediately or in the near future, but
which would have resulted in a kind of socialism similar to that in Yugoslavia, perhaps somewhat more
liberal.

It was for this reason, it seems to me, that the Soviet
Union invaded. Moscow felt that it could not afford

this challenge to the rule of Ulbricht and Gomulka and, indeed, of Brezhnev and Kosygin. This is the sort of thing which the Soviets themselves have declared, and which the Poles have declared as well.

I am quite aware that there were people in Poland, many of them non-Communists, who were afraid that in some way or another Czechoslovakia would not only withdraw from the Warsaw Pact but perhaps would come under the influence of the West. This seems to me to have been neither the desire of the Czechoslovak people or government nor was it likely that it would happen. In any case, it seems to me that the so-called Brezhnev Doctrine, the idea that I suppose a majority of socialist states—defined presumably from Moscow—could intervene in any other state, is, to say the least, the sort of thing that they have criticized in other connections.

CLYDE MARK, Library of Congress: You indicated that the Latin American region was in essence off limits to the Soviet Union. Is there a comparable area that is in essence off limits in Soviet eyes to the United States? Obviously excluding Eastern Europe.

DR. GRIFFITH: Well, I didn't mean to indicate that the United States maintains that Latin America is off limits for the Soviet Union. If so, it would hardly allow the Soviet base in Cuba. It seems to me, in fact, that the willingness of the Eisenhower Administration to allow the establishment of a Soviet military base in Cuba is the point at which things began to go wrong in that respect for American interests. I think that the best corresponding area, in terms of the effective barring of American influence, is Eastern Europe. I would presume that the Soviet Union would like to make this the case in other areas as well. But we would also probably like to make it the case in other areas with respect to the Soviet Union.

The present situation reflects, in essence, the world balance of power, and I don't see that it is likely to change very soon.

After all, the Soviet Union does pay about a million dollars a day to subsidize the Cuban economy. I am not at all sure that if Brazil were suddenly to declare itself Marxist-Leninist and put in for an even greater support that the Soviet Union would really be so anxious to do so. As you may know, Soviet-Cuban relations are not really good. The Soviet Union is opposed to Cuban attempts to start guerrilla movements in Latin America, since it feels they will not be successful. And up to now the Soviet estimate has been more correct than the Cuban. Perhaps one should hope that it continues to be so.

SECOND SESSION

DON BACON, Newhouse Papers: Mr. Rostow, in light of what you know about past Vietnam policy and in light of what you have said in this paper, I wonder if perhaps you would give us your assessment of President Nixon's speech last night.

MR. ROSTOW: The answer to the question is "No." (Laughter.)

WILLIAM EATON, *Chicago Daily News:* Dr. Rostow, I am surprised you can appraise the chances for détente without considering the enormous amount of Soviet military and technical aid that goes into North Vietnam. Doesn't that figure in your détente prognosis?

MR. ROSTOW: Yes. I never was terribly sure precisely what the Soviet calculus was about Vietnam. The history of it is about like this: The Soviet Union undertook not only in 1954 but—more important from the point of view of the 1960s—a wholly unambiguous commitment to make the Laos Accords of 1962 work. More than that, Ambassador Pushkin told Ambassador Harriman that the Soviet Union would undertake to insure the compliance of Hanoi to the Geneva Accords of 1962.

And, as I said on another occasion, my greatest regret about the last eight years is that we didn't make a federal case out of it in the autumn of 1962 when we had clear knowledge that Hanoi was not honoring the Geneva Accords of 1962.

Then there followed a period in which Khrushchev —either giving up on the word passed from Pushkin to Harriman, or finding himself unable to implement it or able to implement his commitment to us only at unacceptable cost in terms of the world Communist movement—was out to lunch on Southeast Asia. When people would talk to Khrushchev in that period, he would act as though he had never heard about Laos, as though it were on some planet beyond Mars.

In 1963-64, South Vietnam began to disintegrate. It started with the Buddhist demonstration in May and accelerated after the assassination of Diem in November. In that setting the North Vietnamese began to put in their regular units, in 1964. The situation was going to hell in a hack. At that point the Russians interested themselves again, notably after Khrushchev was removed. I have no firm evidence; but my general feeling is that Soviet leaders were in Hanoi, early in 1965 not to try to make peace but to cut themselves in on the swag, because they thought that Hanoi was likely to win.

And, of course, the billion dollars or so of Soviet supplies that were granted to North Vietnam in support of the winter-spring offensive of 1967-68 were important and they were planned with knowledge. I should think the arrangements in support of the so-called Tet offensive were made some time around June of 1967.

So the Soviet Union has been in this up to here.

Moreover, I can easily see that Soviet involvement with Hanoi in this enterprise might look like a net advantage to the Soviet Union, given the problems it has posed for us at home and in other parts of the world.

I have also here a feeling on which I cannot put great weight—that after the failure of the winter-spring offensive, after the failure of the Tet offensive, it may be that the Soviet Union may have used whatever margin of influence it has in Hanoi to bring the war towards a negotiated settlement.

I don't believe for a moment that Soviet influence was seriously used in that direction until the winter-spring offensive failed.

There are, moreover, some signs that the Soviet Union is much interested in building up a kind of national presence in Southeast Asia through aid and trade—an area where its logistical capacity is weak. It appears to be acting on somewhat the same basis as it has played a role in the Indian subcontinent; that is, trying to keep the Chinese Communists out.

I go through all this to try to get at the possible evolution through time of Soviet policy. I don't think for a moment Moscow didn't enjoy the discomfiture of the United States in facing this problem. And the struggle could not have gone on in the south without Soviet arms.

But I think it possible that there may have been some changes since the spring of 1968. And I would guess that it is possible—that's the only way I would put it—it's possible that the Soviet Union would like to see the war wound up now and the area pacified, since Hanoi has not been able to hack it and since, for the time being, the inner problems of China absorb Chinese energies.

It may be that they would like to see the area pacified with Moscow emerging with some dilute influence; with the U.S. presence still there, but somewhat diluted; and the Chinese Communists out.

There have been some Soviet articles which are quite extraordinary. They sound like President Johnson's speeches about the New Asia, turned in reverse. What they argue is that Chinese Communist policy, by encouraging this war, has permitted the United States to get its hands on trade with Indonesia and the rest of Southeast Asia, thus building an imperial domain. Those articles evoke all the signs of vitality and co-operation we might evoke in talking about the New Asia. They blame this regional consolidation on a mis-guided Chinese Communist policy of encouraging the war in Vietnam. The argument goes back directly to the protracted Sino-Soviet dispute on what kind of wars of national liberation are legitimate.

I repeat: There has been a critical Soviet role in the war in Southeast Asia—a negative role in failing to honor its commitments to us and to the world com-munity under the Geneva Accords of 1962, which is a very heavy burden the Soviet Union will bear before history; a positive role in supplying an awful lot of hardware to Hanoi.

But, it is also possible that Hanoi's failure in the winter-spring offensive and the opportunity afforded by the cultural revolution and the confusion in China, have led them to a policy in which they may even be encouraging a settlement now, not for sentimental reasons but because they may even have decided: it's very costly; Hanoi isn't going to win; and this is a good time to get a settlement in which they would have a substantial long-run position vis-à-vis China and the United States in Southeast Asia. That is the way I would look at it.

RUSSELL FREEBURG, *Chicago Tribune:* In connection with this New Asia that you are talking about, in the context of some of the remarks you have just made, what should be the United States' role east of Suez after the British pull out? How can this be handled while trying to establish détente with Russia? May this not be a very serious problem for us?

MR. ROSTOW: As I tried to emphasize, the question of détente is a terribly complicated equation.

For reasons I don't fully understand, in the spring of 1967 the Soviet Union saw the Middle East as an area of opportunity. Moscow played some triggering role—as Nasser has pointed out in public—by spreading false information from Syria about an Israeli mobilization on the Syrian border. This information helped get Nasser into the Sinai.

And, in general, we must answer that if they believe they have a great opportunity, they are going to play for it.

Moscow's view may now be different. Having faced all the vicissitudes of working with the Arab world, measuring the costs and the frustrations, Moscow may have come to the conclusion that this is an area in which its best interest is to see some stability. If so— and I am by no means sure—there is a basis for some understanding with Washington.

As for the Gulf area, the best solution would be local

cooperation, notably between Iran and Saudi Arabia. If they could agree, one might see an authentic regional handling of that problem.

More widely, if the Middle East as a whole could develop a spirit of regional cooperation we would all be better off.

So I would hope that the Middle East could handle the Gulf problem substantially on its own. I don't know whether it can. It hinges on some very sensitive collaboration between Saudi Arabia and Iran.

MR. FREEBURG: How about Singapore?

MR. ROSTOW: Singapore, as Lee Kuan Yew never ceases to tell you, depends on the outcome in Vietnam and on the building of a cooperative Asia, including Australia and New Zealand, with United States support, but diminished direct American involvement.

He made a remarkable speech to some of his students who were talking about Vietnam. He said in effect: The United States is buying time for us in Vietnam and if we don't use that time well, we don't deserve to have time bought for us. And that means we have got to collaborate within Asia so that we can prevent further Vietnams.

If you add up the ground forces available in Asia, even with no rearmament of Japan, and match it against what the Chinese Communists have and what they could mount logistically in Southeast Asia, there is plenty of force there if there were a will to pull together. In addition you have had a decade's extraordinary economic and social progress while the Chinese mainland was virtually standing still.

That doesn't mean that the U.S. can pull out with safety for Asia. But Singapore belongs in some sort of a large Asian club, which could do more for itself while we did less; and I think that is what Lee Kuan Yew is saying.

HOWARD HANDLEMAN, U.S. *News & World Report*: You haven't said much yet about Czechoslovakia.

Long range, over the years, how do you think the Czech experience and Czech events will affect the chances of détente between the United States and the Soviet Union, or will they affect them at all?

MR. ROSTOW: Well, they already have. They have slowed up the missile talks. They have slowed up the passage of the non-proliferation treaty. And they have laid before the world a doctrine that virtually vetoes the United Nations Charter for nations with Communist regimes.

We already have paid a heavy cost.

The rather somber tone of my argument about détente as a whole results from the Czech affair; although I have always tended to be cautious about the pace of détente. Some of you may recall a piece I did in *Foreign*

Affairs called "The Third Round," warning against excessive optimism in 1963 at the time of the test ban treaty.

But the Czech affair should give us all pause. If you assume that Soviet policy is going to remain the way it was in Czechoslovakia—namely, that Dubcek's degree of assertiveness and liberalism was enough for Russia to feel itself so threatened that it had to put troops in—then I think the prospects for détente would be very black. This is so because on any objective assessment, the forces of nationalism and liberalism in Eastern Europe are going to gather strength, and heavy-industry patterns for organizing the economy are going to get more and more out of date.

So if you assume Soviet policy is constant and you assume these trends persist, one must conclude Eastern Europe will become increasingly explosive. And you are not going to have détente. You are going to have a very dangerous world.

But we need not despair, for Soviet policy could change, as it did from time to time in the pre-1914 decade. There is a kind of Czarist quality now to Soviet leaders' anxiety about liberalism at home and in Eastern Europe. And there are phases in Russian history of very rigid autocracy and anxiety; but also phases of relative liberalism at home and indications even of tolerance for liberalism abroad.

We need not necessarily assume that there will be no rethinking of what is livable for the Soviet Union in terms of assertiveness and liberalism in Eastern Europe. But if you conclude that Russia will never let an Eastern European country up to the levels of nationalism and liberalism of the Dubcek regime, then I think you would have to predict very dark times ahead, because I believe those forces are on the rise historically, generation by generation.

MR. HANDLEMAN: Would you make that prediction?

MR. ROSTOW: No. I have a little more faith. I would not make the assumption because I think that Soviet policy will move in a way to permit higher degrees of liberalization in Eastern Europe with the passage of time.

I have always looked at East-West relations on a very long time horizon. If you start with Stalin's time—say, with Molotov walking out of Paris in July of 1947—and see where we are now, 22 years later, the direction of movement is hopeful. It's slow and painful. But I think that is the direction in which things will continue to go.

That is why I refuse to say flatly that present Soviet dispositions are permanent. But if they were, then we would be up against a very tough proposition.

JAMES McCARTNEY, Knight Newspapers: How

do you assess the possibilities for peace in Vietnam?

MR. ROSTOW: None of this is off the record is it? I don't want to discuss peace in Vietnam. I just don't want to get into it.

JOHN OSBORNE, *New Republic:* A point of history, Professor Rostow. As of January 19, forgetting what has happened since, did you feel that our government had in hand a set of formulated, defined, coherent terms with which to go into serious negotiations in Paris if and when such negotiations became possible?

MR. ROSTOW: Yes. (Laughter.)

RAOUL KULBERG, Institute of Sino-Soviet Studies, The George Washington University: Professor Rostow, you mentioned Soviet violation of the UN Charter with regard to Czechoslovakia and that sort of thing. I wonder if you see a role in the general pattern, not necessarily only in détente, but in the world, for the UN in the political security area? Will its role be limited more to cultural and economic development? What role, if any, do you see the UN effectively playing, or is it going to be playing one, in your estimation?

MR. ROSTOW: I think the UN is playing an important role. One of the problems in talking about the UN is that people talk about it as *The* UN. The UN is an Assembly, it's a Security Council; it's ECO-SOC; it's Regional Commissions; it's many other bodies. You don't really see how much the UN is doing unless you start with our national policy and see how many components of that national policy have a UN dimension.

But I don't want to evade your central point, which is major and legitimate.

We all started with the hope that the security problems of the world would be solved by the continuation of the wartime alliance of the Soviet Union, the United States, Britain and France and China.

Many things may have contributed to Stalin's calculus, but in fact he opted for a different counsel. In a speech in February 1946, he announced that wasn't going to happen. There was not going to be concord. There was going to be implacable hostility from Moscow. And there was.

Therefore we went off to build pacts and other forms of blocking strength around the world. In the meanwhile we dealt with the Communist world as best we could, using the UN machinery in a wide variety of pragmatic ways where it could be used.

Now, let's assume the best: a non-proliferation treaty; a missile pact; parallelism in the Middle East; parallelism in South Asia and Southeast Asia. If you have parallelism in the regions and serious works on arms control at the center, then you would be some distance back towards the original San Francisco concept of the UN. That is what it would have been if it had worked.

I was assuming with maximum hope, that after rousting about for a generation or two and coming to realize that this is a world of diffusing power which is not going to take form as anybody's empire and coming to realize that it is also a dangerous world, dangerous for the Soviet Union as well as for everybody else—Moscow might come back to square one, with something like the spirit and intent of San Francisco. You can see bits, you can see glimpses occasionally, moments in diplomacy, of what the world would look like. And it's very attractive. Very attractive. But we're not there. The UN obviously, then, could be used very fully.

CHALMERS ROBERTS, *The Washington Post:* Walt, the present administration is telling us that while you were in the White House the Soviet Union was developing an SS-9 (intercontinental ballistic missile) and this weapon is being interpreted by the Secretary of Defense, currently, as indicative of thoughts about a first strike. Was this in fact the judgment in the administration you served? And if so, why didn't you tell us about it? And what would be its effect on détente?

MR. ROSTOW: I'm not going to get into it, Chal. I'd love to give you the story, but not tonight.

MR. ROBERTS: Well, weapons have to do with détente.

MR. ROSTOW: Yes.

MR. ROBERTS: First strike has to do with détente.

How can you talk about détente without talking about these things?

MR. ROSTOW: Well, I am assuming that we have some margin of safety now and with the development of things that are going forward or could go forward, we can maintain a reliable second-strike capability and continue to render a first strike irrational.

Now, that doesn't mean that along the way you won't have technological developments of one kind or another and adjustments. But that was my underlying assumption. It's not one that I felt necessary—nor do I now feel it necessary—to defend in terms of particular pieces of hardware.

MR. ROBERTS: Your assumption in the limited ABM system proposed by President Johnson did not include, at least the public assumption, to my recollection, did not include this factor.

MR. ROSTOW: I don't want to get into debates on the SS-9. But you should know one of the things that was considered was the role of a limited ABM system in defending hardened Minuteman sites. But I honestly think, Chal, that what you're talking about is a technically legitimate range of issues for détente which are inevitably involved in maintaining over a period of time a reliable second-strike capability. And that is how, hopefully you render irrational a first strike. I repeat what I said. I think that you are inevitably going to have debates on particular phases of the arms race, especially since the nuclear arms race is not under negotiated control. But I do not think that getting into the fine points of particular pieces of hardware is an essential element in a paper of this kind. It's an interesting question but I'm not going to get into it.

MR. ROBERTS: Now, you can't get off the hook that easy. (Laughter.)

MR. ROSTOW: I sure can. It's the easiest thing in the world, Chal.

MR. ROBERTS: You proposed last year sitting down with the Russians to discuss the missile race, offensive and defensive weapons. Right?

MR. ROSTOW: You mean President Johnson's proposal?

MR. ROBERTS: Yes, the administration you served. And you must have had this factor somewhere in your considerations.

MR. ROSTOW: There was thoroughly responsible preparation of our position. (Laughter.)

JAMES L. YEUNGER, *Chicago Tribune:* You were speaking about how Western Europe felt Gaullism or France may recede as a major impediment to European unity. I have just returned from several weeks in Europe and several people told me that Gaullism was not only De Gaulle. They noted the current trouble with a number of attempts at inter-country cooperation. In view of that and in view of African tribal conflicts and Latin American nationalism, I was wondering whether you might be a little too optimistic about the chances for this stability, interdependence, cooperation taking place, even though De Gaulle is not a part of the scene?

MR. ROSTOW: I tried to give my paper as much a sense of the possibility of failure as the possibility of success. I don't think any of these constructive developments are predestined. So far as Gaullism is concerned, I tried not to hinge my article on De Gaulle. I said whether Europe moves post-De Gaulle. The paper was written before De Gaulle departed the scene; but I wouldn't change it.

I have not been in Western Europe for some time but I did find it striking when I was last there, to find men like Franz Josef Strauss, talking openly—along these lines. He said, what De Gaulle demonstrated to us in Europe, was that a country of 50 million, no matter how talented and technically gifted, is incapable of making a serious dent on the problems we face.

In any case, the conclusion—I have the feeling that a second wave—perhaps not as exalted as the first—towards European unity is under way. Having had the full challenge for a protracted period of a devil's advocate against, if you like, Monnet, de Gasperi, and Schuman, the Europeans are coming back to a realization that, in fact, European unity is the only way. I don't know whether it's going to happen. What I am saying is that I think I can see the bases for such a second wave. I know the strands of thought in Europe which make the burial of President Kennedy's July 4th, 1962, Interdependence Speech somewhat premature. If you look at that speech, you will find he took a long perspective. I think it's going to be proved right. But it's a matter of faith. If some argue it won't happen because of inertia, lack of will, and old-fashioned nationalism, I would respond: you could well be right. But if I was a betting man, I would say Britain is going into the Common Market in the next three years; and I'd take a 50-50 bet on it.

LEON HERMAN, Library of Congress: Professor Rostow, in your calculus of the chances for a détente, what importance do you assign to the Soviet doctrine that a great power keeps only those agreements it wishes to keep and not the others, of which the Laos agreement was probably a good example?

MR. ROSTOW: That's why I raised the point about the Geneva Accords of 1962 in my *Times* interview.

I said then I was not putting this point to score on the past but looking to the future. Hopefully, we are going to have a missile agreement. And, if there is anything I've got to commend to my fellow citizens out of experience since 1945 it is: Make a federal case immediately out of the slightest deviation from an agreement with a Communist power.

MR. ROBERTS: Why didn't you make a federal case out of Laos?

MR. ROSTOW: Maybe I'll put that in a book sometime. I'm not going to discuss it now. But let me say one thing about Laos because it does bear on what is the gut issue here in general.

The fundamental problem of Laos of 1962 was the problem that Tocqueville describes when he discusses the underlying weaknesses of democracies in military affairs and diplomacy. He says that the democracies are so taken up with their economic and domestic concerns that they only turn to major security issues late, but when they do turn, and that becomes the central national enterprise, they become more effective, he says, than autocracies. It's awfully hard from a standing start, when you have what may look like a minor affair, to take on—to initiate—a major crisis. That is a weakness which we've corrected to some extent, as we've learned some of the lessons of the 1930s. But we haven't been as strict and responsive as we ought to be about agreements.

WILLIAM K. WYANT, *St. Louis Post-Dispatch*: You have seen that several times in our newspaper we have raised the question whether this country as a society will be able to stand the force of this difficult world we're living in. Could you tell us whether or not in any sense this question came up in the Johnson Administration, perhaps in connection with the Vietnam war, and expand on it a bit?

MR. ROSTOW: I have been concerned about this problem all the way back to *The Stages of Economic Growth,* that is, with what happens to a society when it comes to the stage of mass affluence which, in effect, was Marx's definition of communism. Marx's definition of communism, as you may remember, was the time when scarcity was lifted from man. He had a rather happy nineteenth century view that when scarcity was lifted from man his better nature would flower.

That is one possibility. There are others less attractive about which I speculated a decade ago. Incidentally, the phrase The New Frontier arose out of that question. But I don't know the answer. We are not yet so affluent a society that all our people, by any means, have all the food, shelter, clothing, housing, education, health that they want; but enough people are beginning to have these things, and beginning to take them for granted, to raise the question. And there are other parts of the world where you can see the same phenomenon.

I have no doubt in my own mind that it's worth the human race going forward to find out whether affluent man can make a decent life without the pressures and challenges of scarcity.

As children are born in the world the simple judgment one can make is that they deserve in their life the best education, health, and food that you can give them, the best chance to express their God-given talents.

But clearly—thus far—affluence has raised as many problems as it has solved. These new problems have brought about the recurrence of an older pattern of thought about foreign policy.

In the 1930s many said: Why bother about abroad? We've got big problems at home. There was both a right-wing and a left-wing American political isolationist view in the 1930s. Harry Hopkins had it in an early stage; Herbert Hoover articulated it; and both in almost identical terms.

Especially when the world is murky and you don't have something as simple as Stalin going after you with a baseball bat, people say, well—you know—it won't be too bad to pull out; and we've got a lot to do at home.

MORTON KONDRACKI, *Chicago Sun-Times:* What do you think the possibilities are for the development of a European regional nuclear deterrent, and what are the implications of that?

MR. ROSTOW: Under the non-proliferation treaty, that could only come about if there were a sovereign

Europe. That is not excluded. That is, if Europe were to become a sovereign state, then it would have the right to become a nuclear Europe. What is ruled out is what is called a loose European affair, nuclear affair.

I think that the European nuclear problem has diminished since the Cuban missile crisis. It was important from 1958 and the beginning of Khrushchev's Berlin ultimatum down through the whole nuclear blackmail phase of Soviet policy which ended with the Cuban missile crisis. The whole question of Europe's role in the nuclear business was a major issue at that time. But it seeped away after that. It would be revived only if the United States were to go into such a paroxysm of isolationism or quasi-isolationism that Europeans would begin to think they were in mortal danger. It could revive quickly under that impulse, plus some pressure from the Russians; but for the moment it's latent. So long as the United States is steady, the European nuclear problem is what you might call an insurance policy problem. It's a problem of having enough know-how in hand—technology and maybe a few bombs—so that if the United States really went into a policy of withdrawal, they'd have the foundations for moving forward rather rapidly to a reputable nuclear deterrent of their own. But right now I don't regard the question as hot. Others may disagree with me.

MR. EATON: Dr. Rostow, at the time of the bombing halt last November, there was a widespread impression—and the White House I think contributed to it—that the Soviets would guarantee the understanding that there would be no shelling of cities, no use of the demilitarized zone. Since then there have been, obviously, many violations of that. Do you think that's another area where the White House or Washington should make a federal case out of the Soviet lack of follow-through?

MR. ROSTOW: I won't go into what our communications were with the Soviet Union, but the Soviet Union did not guarantee those understandings. The understandings were between us and Hanoi. The question of what we do is up to us, in the case of violations.

MR. EATON: There wasn't any Soviet—

MR. ROSTOW: I won't go into what there was, but I'm saying that this was not like Pushkin and Harriman.

HAROLD EBERLE, Office of Representative Robert J. Corbett: It does seem like this gentleman has a point with his question on the SS-9, since it goes to one of your points, on reasons to expect a détente. If I am not mistaken, you said that Russian military doctrine and its weapons were being shaped for something short of conflict, and the administration is telling us the opposite. We've either got to hear the administration is wrong or you're going to have to modify your point, aren't you?

MR. ROSTOW: No. I don't have to modify it. What I was saying was that the Soviet Union operated for a long time on very much what you might call a 1950s, U.S. basic national security policy paper, namely, that any military contact with the United States was tantamount to general nuclear war and had to be avoided.

Now after the Cuban missile crisis, there were certain debates and changes in Soviet military doctrine which, for the first time, would admit the possibility of limited Soviet-U.S. military contact without a nuclear war. I did not say that they had, therefore, abandoned their efforts to build up their own nuclear capabilities. There was an add-on, just as, if you like, President Kennedy's time, the buildup of conventional forces, airlift and sealift, was an add-on which was accompanied by a very big expansion in our second strike nuclear capability via Polaris and Minutemen.

I may have not been lucid, but the point I was making was that there has been a significant change since the Cuban missile crisis in Soviet military doctrine. There has also been a significant increase in Soviet nuclear offensive capabilities and some increase in ABM capabilities. These two things have grown concurrently.

I was not addressing myself to the second problem.

The fact that they changed their doctrines and, to some extent increased certain conventional capabilities, does not mean that they have thereby cut down their nuclear capabilities.

MR. EBERLE: Their doctrine now is specifically, if I understand it from some of the writings of the chief of staff of the Russian forces, that they must be in a position to be able to deliver a crushing blow to the imperialist powers. The administration is telling us that with the buildup of these weapons, and it has been dramatic in the last six or seven months and projected on ahead, they have exceeded parity now and are going into superiority. Isn't that correct?

MR. ROSTOW: I haven't followed the latest testimony before the Congress; and I don't know how you measure parity. I have no doubt at all that there has been a radical buildup of Soviet offensive, nuclear capabilities, plus a modest buildup of ABM capabilities, plus some increase in conventional forces, especially in their mobility, plus a change in basic doctrine, which does not exclude military contact with the United States on a limited-war basis. All these things have happened.

But I haven't seen the detailed testimony of the Department of Defense on how it rates current Soviet relative capabilities or what criteria it uses to rate them. And I'm not going to get into the numbers.

But I would say that Soviet military doctrine is some-what more sophisticated than the notion of simply "a crushing blow against the imperialist powers." They've done some fine-grained analysis of the cost both ways of a full nuclear exchange; they talk about limited wars; and they also talk about wars of national liberation.

They are capable of writing about military matters without that kind of May 1st rhetoric. That doesn't mean there's any the less danger. (Laughter.)

JOSEPH WHELAN, Library of Congress: I wonder if, Professor Rostow, you would comment on the con-tradiction that U.S. intervention in Korea was justified, as correct and in the U.S. interest and yet intervention in Vietnam is not justified as correct but said to be contrary to U.S. interests?

MR. ROSTOW: I think it's a little hard to see ex-actly what the argument would look like. You said, "Here's an argument that Korea's okay and North Vietnam's not okay." On what is it based? I don't know how the argument would be put, on what ground the distinction would be made.

MR. WHELAN: That's my question. On what ground would they make such a distinction?

MR. ROSTOW: I have found with most ardent Viet-nam people that when you've gone through three, four, or five hours and they've gotten all the things off their chest and they've finally got some alleged member of the establishment that they can really tell off—and you tell them back—and what it comes down to is they don't care what happens to Asia. Suppose they do cut each other's throats or China takes them over? That's where you really end up. There is no argument that I have heard that has really held up under the strain of three, four, or five-hour debates, alleging Korea was okay but Vietnam wasn't.

CLYDE MARK, Library of Congress: In your discussion of areas where you thought the United States should encourage regionalism, you left out the Middle East. What is the future of this area? Do you think, for example, that Russia will achieve hegemony over the Middle East? Should the United States promote regionalism there or should the Middle East be neutralized as you suggested for Asia? Let's define the Middle East as stretching from Morocco to Iran and Turkey to the Somali Republic.

MR. ROSTOW: I wasn't thinking of the sweep all the way to Morocco. But I did suggest rather tersely that this extremely tangled area would do better for itself if it could somehow overcome the three major schisms which have bedeviled its life and made it the object of intervention and intrusion and manipulation: First, the Arab-Israeli; second, the radical versus moderate Arabs; and, third, the Arabs versus the other

Moslems, notably Iran and Turkey.

I think that if they could come to the judgment that the central task they face in finding dignity for their culture in a modern world—because that is their problem and it's a problem I have real compassion for—is not throwing Israel into the sea or fighting among themselves but going to work together to elevate the life of their people.

They've got marvelous resources. I find Iraq a heartbreaking place to study because it has oil and it has sulphur, water and land but it's getting nowhere serious in its development.

Jordan did better from 1957 to 1967 than anyone thought possible with virtually no resources; and there are a lot more people in the Middle East who would like to do this and free themselves from these painful, obsessive memories and policies than one would usually credit, given the net vector of their policy. But until you get the beginnings of a settlement of this war, I think that it's somewhat unlikely. And I myself do not see at the moment the way through, given the nature of the politics in Cairo, the politics of the fedayeen, and the politics of Israel itself. Somewhere, however, I've got a residue of hopefulness which is hard to sustain in face of the day-to-day facts. It stems from an historical pattern. We have had in the postwar world a series of leaders, some Communist, some non-

Communist, who, having come out of colonialism or what they regarded as a quasi-colonial setting, have launched out into the world, have taken the memories of intrusion and humiliation from the past and, instead of ploughing them into the modernization of their society, they have gone out into their region somewhat the way the French did after the Revolution. After the French survived the counter-revolutionaries, they began to get rather big ideas about the extension of the French Revolution in Europe; then Napoleon took it all the way to Moscow before Europe saw the end of it.

We have seen that pattern before in the wake of revolutionary situations—a phase of evangelistic expansionism, at the cost of neglect of the welfare of the society. And we should not be too condescending about it, because there was a good deal of that spirit when the United States went up to Canada during the War of 1812; and I don't think we've ever quite gotten over the fact that the Canadians didn't really want to buy our version of independence and our revolution. It's a phase.

Now, this is the problem of Castro. He doesn't want to grow sugar, he really doesn't. If you read his speeches, it's clear he yearns to get up there in the Andes and make it the Sierra Maestra of Latin America, although, in fact, the takeover of Cuba was in Havana, not out in the countryside.

You had Ben Bella and you had Nkrumah, you had Sukarno and you have Nasser and you've got Mao himself and you have Ho—all men who have a vision in their mind of achieving a kind of local empire. In Mao's case it's a pretty big empire including a good chunk of Siberia and the lands and peoples all the way down to Djakarta.

It's the reaction of men who have come through a revolution; whose nations have suffered authentic intrusions and humiliations. Instead of drawing the lesson that the way to find dignity is by getting to work and making a modern society so folks who had their industrial revolution 20, 30, 40, or 100 years earlier are not going to push them around, they turn outward.

Each of these men has a map in his head. Mao has passed the map out to every school child in China. It's a pretty chilling map. And Ho carries a vision that, no matter what he signed in 1954 or what he signed in 1962, it is legitimate for him to take over the old French colonial empire in Asia.

Sukarno had a map and Ben Bella. Castro has described his vision often and in compelling terms. If you can draw back from and look at it as a novelist—in simple terms—it is not hard to see how men, having gone through their experience, might fetch up with that kind of a view.

To come back to the Middle East, various other leaders have played on Nasser's schizophrenia: I say schizophrenia because Nasser had some serious plans for his country, but he never could stay with them long enough. He just had to get involved in the Yemen or some other affair to try to make this map come true—the map of an Arab world which would be run from Cairo.

These men are part of the history; but I think a fading part of the history. They are a part of the past. They are passing from the world scene for two reasons.

First, in going abroad, they ran into other peoples' nationalism. They didn't always run into a buzzsaw like Israel but they ran into one form of serious resistance or another. And at home, the fact that they get involved abroad, meant they had to neglect the welfare of the people. For a time large dreams and zenophobic speeches sufficed. But in the end frustration abroad and stagnation at home will push them into the past; although all of them are not yet out of power.

This is a long way around; and I'm sorry to have taken so much time. But if I have any hope for the Middle East finding its way forward, it doesn't derive from anything I know about current diplomacy. I hope—and I am sure—diplomacy is very active. I hope we get a diplomatic breakthrough, although I don't see its shape, given, as I say, the best perception I can have of the political forces with which some of the Arab leaders are dealing and Israel is dealing.

Nevertheless, I don't lose hope because I do not believe the Middle East is exempt from the forces whereby these men give way to more pragmatic leaders—less ambitious abroad—who get on with the job of building more modern nations at home.

THIRD SESSION

MR. ROSTOW: Now a bit about optimism and pessimism.

I begin with two strands of pessimism. I begin by assuming that we live in the most dangerous half century in which man has ever lived. Three things have converged to make world war the normal historical outcome of what we have faced.

The three elements are these: a great ideological conflict; a world (embracing Latin America, Africa, the Middle East, and Asia) which has the same capacity to trigger major conflict that the Balkans did before 1914; that is, nations unformed, in transition, explosive in themselves, vulnerable to intrusion, lying across important areas of power; and, then, you have nuclear weapons.

I begin, therefore, with an exceedingly somber view of what the task is of human survival. And, as I look back at the first quarter century of the human effort to survive in this environment, I am respectful of the achievement, the great negative achievement; namely, that we have avoided major war.

Second, I have always been extremely cautious about the long-run possibilities of United States-Soviet relations. The historical depth of the problem of the Soviet Union's relation to Eastern Europe and Germany, the historical depth of the problem of arms control and inspection, have led me to believe that benign change will come very slowly. The changes that have to take place within the Soviet Union—in its view of the world and in its society—before it can come to a true ending of the cold war, go deep.

On the other hand, the critical importance to the human race of these issues has led me to be willing to give a good part of my time and effort to helping us take small steps forward in that direction.

A good deal of what passes for optimism stems simply from being pleased and surprised at the limited things that have been accomplished against this somber background.

But there may be more to it than that.

One of the things I have learned from history and active life is that what turns out to be critically important at a certain time, looked at five years later may not be what men at the time thought to be critically important.

Therefore, in any current situation you have to look at what is and face it sharply, even masochistically; but you also have to look at the dynamic forces at work and look for those forces which might, in time, improve your situation. If you find them, you must commit yourself to nurturing them.

In short, my view is not one of passive optimism or pessimism, it is operational.

I have seen many situations of objectively short-run pessimism turned around by action based on possibilities not immediately obvious; for example, the Battle of the Atlantic in 1942-43; the long-range fighter and air supremacy over Germany in 1943-44; the resilience of the younger generation in Western Europe, in collaboration with the men who knew the world before 1914, in the Marshall Plan period; the unexpected determination of the younger generation of South Koreans in the 1960s; the generally better performance in economic development of non-Communist than Communist underdeveloped nations; etc.

In other words, I believe it proper to start, as Professor Griffith did, with the most hardminded, unforgiving analysis of what the problems are you are up against. There is danger in underestimating your problems. But there is an equal danger in underestimating the assets which you might have if you isolate and work with those assets; and the assets may not be obvious. In five years, if you do your job, they will be the conventional wisdom; but at the time that you have to make your dispositions, they may be hard to find.

It has been my experience, over a long period—and I could have cited further examples—that there is quite often a gap between the sharp critics' assessment of prospects at a particular moment of time and what the situation might be if you look deeper at things which may not be palpable and then act on them.

Now a final word about the problem of peace. A distinguished American economic historian named John Nef has made this point: in the eighteenth century men came to a concept of limited war, even though they were struggling over the great stakes of empire that were opened up by the age of discovery as well as over the European power balance. Then came the Industrial Revolution. The Industrial Revolution, for a time, made war worse, as it put greater physical power in the hands of the ambitious. Some were led to dreams of total power—which yielded wars where the full power of industrialization was applied to killing and physical destruction. Something may be happening now in the world which could change the character of war in the long run, just as fear of atomic weapons has imposed self-restraint, thus far, in the short run.

What is happening is that the objects of war, the weaker regions of the world, are clearly becoming less vulnerable to manipulation as they modernize and begin slowly to assume a firm, modern character.

This is my first and, I think in the end, my most

important comment on Professor Griffith's paper.

If you are going to have not merely two powers in the world—or not even only an industrialized Atlantic North—but if the soft areas which were bypassed by industrialization earlier harden up (Latin America, Africa, the Middle East, and Southern Asia), there may come about a general awareness that the fruits of war can no longer be world dominion, or European dominion, or Asian dominion.

There may come about a gradual awareness that war may be more dangerous than advantageous, as its advantages and possibilities diminish and the dangers rise.

In fact, something like this sense is growing in parts of the world.

As we go through what I am sure will be, in the next generation, a most dangerous passage—when all manner of mortal dangers can be envisaged as realistically possible—I would like not to rule out as impossible the finding of some sort of greater inherent stability.

But I fully agree with Professor Griffith that we face many hurdles and dangers in trying to get from here to there. . . .

DR. GRIFFITH: The public, I assume, conceives the present policy of the administration to be to get out of the war as rapidly as possible in consonance with national security.

MR. ROSTOW: When was that not the policy? (Laughter.)

DR. GRIFFITH: The question is not whether it was the policy, Walt, the question is to what extent it was believed.

I don't think that as many people believed that the Johnson Administration was trying to get out of the war as urgently as they think the present administration is. I think that this reflects no particular credit on either administration; public opinion has changed in this respect.

Now, what I fear is that the war will drag on for some time. I find it difficult to see why Hanoi should give in now when it can so easily imagine that it can wait and will get better terms, rather than make peace now.

DAVID MARTIN, United States Senate Staff, Office of Senator Thomas Dodd: Dr. Griffith, I have a couple of questions bearing on the poll, some of which are not very meaningful because it depends on the questions they ask.

There was a poll dated approximately March 21st, I believe. The questions asked on that occasion were somewhat more meaningful. They asked them whether they thought we ought to pull out immediately and

26 percent said Yes.

They asked whether they thought we ought to step up the war in an effort to win it and 32 percent said they were in favor of stepping up the tempo of the war in an effort to win militarily.

They asked them whether we ought to continue doing what we're doing now and 19 percent said Yes and the balance were in favor of getting out but they had no strong feelings about getting out immediately.

What this amounted to was that 75 percent of the American people, again, were prepared to go along at least with what we are doing now and a substantial percentage were prepared to go along with a lot more than we are doing now.

I do feel that the public opinion is frequently misread because of the noisiness of the opposition to the war.

DR. GRIFFITH: Let me repeat what I said about the Vietnam war. It is simply that I do not think that we have won the war. I think we have not won it and I do not think the majority of the American people are prepared, as your poll would indicate, to try to win it.

What they seem to want is some kind of a compromise. Now, as I indicated, I am as much opposed as Walt Rostow is to unilateral withdrawal. It seems to me that would be a disaster for the United States.

But I, regretfully, have come to the conclusion that whether or not we could win the war, and up to now we have, it seems to me, in the last year probably done somewhat better than we had been doing before—it is quite clear, and I think this is a judgment to which the new administration has come more clearly than the previous one, that the American people are not prepared in a majority to put up the energy and blood and treasure that would be required to win it.

Furthermore, I think that the war has very seriously split the American public and, although I would myself certainly not share the view of those 26 percent who want to get out, it is, I think, significant that this 26 percent includes—and I realize that I am subject here to the charge of speaking from the geographic deformation of Cambridge, Massachusetts—

(Laughter.)

It is, I think, true that this 26 percent includes an overwhelming majority of the educated youth of the country, at least a much greater majority than would be the case in other parts of the population.

I think that there is a massive alienation in this respect which, deplore it or not—and I happen to—one still has to take into account, and therefore I think that one of the best arguments for following a policy of bringing the war to a conclusion is that the damage it has done to domestic consensus is already extremely great and will increase.

RUSSELL FREEBURG, *Chicago Tribune*: Professor Griffith, could I ask both you and Dr. Rostow, when you talk about unilateral withdrawal, are you against any unilateral withdrawal, say, 50,000 or 100,000 troops by the end of this year or are you talking about just pulling everything out?

DR. GRIFFITH: I was not talking about pulling everything out. I am, myself, in favor, if we cannot bring about mutual withdrawals, of a small unilateral withdrawal of the kind you speak, perhaps 50,000 men, in order to encourage the Saigon government to the view that it should play a larger role in the war than it has.

But I am very much opposed to total unilateral withdrawal.

MR. FREEBURG: Dr. Rostow, would you answer that?

MR. ROSTOW: The issue of pulling some U.S. forces out of South Vietnam was first raised publicly at the National Press Club, I believe, by General Westmoreland when he was home in November of 1967.

He said that within two years he thought that the South Vietnamese would be far enough forward so that some U.S. forces could be withdrawn. Westmoreland's judgment of 1967 may prove accurate.

And General Johnson, the Chief of Staff of the Army, made a similar statement after his trip to Vietnam a little later.

President Johnson always refused to make a judgment on this because he had no decision to make at the moment; although he felt that the men in the field had a right to assessment about the future. He just didn't have the knowledge to make a confident assessment about the future. And no one was asking him to make a decision at that time.

I feel the same way now. It depends, of course, on the level of infiltration and on the forces that are mounted against the South Vietnamese. If the level of those forces, the level of infiltration remains tolerably low and the situation in I Corps is relatively quiet and secure—if the DMZ remains relatively quiet with the bombing cessation relative to what it was in 1966, 1967 —it's possible but I think it's got to be made as a practical military decision on practical grounds.

May I also make a statement about winning the war. Winning the war, in my time in government, was always defined in terms of three things:

First—and perhaps in the end more important for Southeast Asia than anything else—the re-establishment of the Geneva Accords on Laos of 1962 and the effective monitoring of those accords, because it's Laos which is the route to Thailand and the rest of Southeast Asia.

Second, the re-establishment of the DMZ, leaving the question of unification open to the peoples of North Vietnam and of South Vietnam without compulsion, in peace.

And, third, a political determination on the basis of one-man-one-vote in the South concerning their political future!

That has, at least in my understanding, constituted the victory that we sought. That is in my understanding the concept of nailing the coonskin to the wall. I don't know of any military man or civilian, under the terms in which this war was fought, who set any other goals, and, as nearly as I know, they still remain the goals.

And so I have always found it puzzling when someone put on one side the concept of winning a victory and on the other side the concept of negotiation, because if we're going to get to the re-establishment of the Geneva Accords of 1962 and we're going to get a well-monitored DMZ and we're going to arrange for a one-man-one-vote election, including those who are now fighting with the VC and get the non-South Vietnamese troops on both sides home, we've got to talk about it. And that's presumably why there have been efforts to get talks going for as long as we put troops in there.

There is no point kicking dead horses around. It may be fun to hold up the image of some fellow who thought we were going to go up to the Red River Delta and occupy the place; but that is not the way the war has been fought.

If something else is in mind other than those three objectives, I think we ought to be explicit about it.

BENJAMIN F. SCHEMMER, President and Publisher, *Journal of the Armed Forces:* Professor Rostow, as you today weigh our progress towards those definitions of a win in South Vietnam, would you comment on which, if any, of the political constraints imposed on the battlefield commanders in that theater during 1966 and 1967 you feel might better have not been imposed, given the benefit of hindsight?

MR. ROSTOW: I'm not going to discuss that.

STEPHEN BANKER, Canadian Broadcasting Corporation: Mr. Rostow, might I invite you to linger somewhat more than you did before on a point that Mr. Griffith raised, namely, the effect of foreign policy on the domestic scene and the disruptive events on the campus of today—you have been on a campus recently —and also the rising temper of the black community.

And, as an adjunct to that question, I ask you whether you agree with those observers who think that anti-Americanism around the world is now at some kind of high and whether, if so, some attempt should be made to placate that rather nebulous idea of world opinion?

MR. ROSTOW: On the first point I call to your attention my analysis of the consequences of pulling out after our commitment has been made.

I began with the consequences of such withdrawal for our own society—the debate in our society, a debate between the right and the left with the deepest kinds of recriminations, for having fought a war and not seen it through to an honorable conclusion with all the subsequent consequences for our alliances.

I believe the strains we would go through under those circumstances are very much greater than the strains which we are now experiencing.

Second, although Vietnam is often evoked, I think that the problem of black and white techniques of confrontation, which you are talking about, have very little to do with the war in Vietnam and I don't think they would automatically subside if we got peace in Vietnam.

Vietnam may be brought into the arguments for those techniques. And, mind you, I'm not denying great uneasiness about the war in Vietnam. I've got great uneasiness about it. No one feels good about a war.

But I call to your attention my judgment that the end of war in Vietnam will not automatically solve the problem of allocations of resources for civil purposes. I don't think Vietnam is the magic key; although we all pray for peace for its own sake. I don't want to go into my own analysis of the temper of the students— of the extremists, white and black. It would take us too far afield.

Now, as for the United States and the world, as near as I can make out, ever since the United States came back onto the world scene with the Truman Doctrine, the world has vacillated between two views of the United States:

One—that we're a great big power that's going to get them into a big war;

And, two—that we're likely to go home and leave them undefended.

I remember very well what the reactions of some were to the Truman Doctrine; this is a militaristic doctrine; we're defending a corrupt government; we're getting ourselves overextended in the world.

There are passages of famous columnists that one can extract about Greece in 1947 that are virtually identical with passages about Korea and identical with passages on Vietnam. And so also with editorials in certain newspapers.

And then President Truman's posture came into better balance with the Marshall Plan.

But in Asia right now I'm sure the underlying concern with the United States is that we'll pull out too fast; and beneath the surface in a great deal of Europe that is the underlying concern, not necessarily the concern of the most vociferous people, but the underlying concern of a great majority of those who think about the world and their future.

They know well that, if we prove unreliable in an alliance, having invested 500,000 men and taken the casualties we have, that the pulling out under these circumstances will be the breaking of the nerve of American society; and they stand in fear of it.

The Israelis know this. Most Europeans know this in their hearts.

I have watched, with all due respect, the vacillations of opinion in Canada. A certain number of people watch international politics as an observer sport. But if you're undertaking responsibilities in your own interest and the interest of others, I think you've got to pay a lot of attention to those who feel their vital interests are involved: to the participant players not the observers.

There's a natural law that's observable in government the degree of philosophy and "statesmanship" that one finds during a particular crisis is inversely related to the distance of the country from the place in trouble.

When Berlin is in trouble, Europe is really quite interested. In the Punta del Este Conference of 1962, when we voted Cuba out of the OAS club, the West

Coast countries—Chile, Peru, and so on—were rather "statesmanlike"; and so was Argentina. But for those who lived in the Caribbean area—and it didn't make any difference whether it was democratic Costa Rica or some other state—Cuba and the problems it raised were taken right seriously.

I won't comment directly about Canada's views.

But for the United States this is mighty serious business. We've taken a lot of casualties in this quarter-century. We've carried a lot of strain. And many nations enjoy their independence and their liberty and their affluence because the people of the United States undertook these responsibilities—not because we're interested in empire, but because we felt the cost of not taking them would be greater. And that's the case in Vietnam.

I don't regard myself as a great pundit on American opinion; although I've seen the polls. But I will tell you that one of the abiding conclusions I have drawn from having been in government is an enormous respect for the steadiness of the people of our country.

They have had a large part of the media—the most effective part of the media—hammering away against the government's Vietnam policy. They've had to live with war in their living room, with their children present every night; and war is just as ugly as sin.

They have had to deal with a war where there was

no fixed front so they couldn't see whether things were going badly or they couldn't see whether things were going well.

There were statistics issued; but these statistics were often mocked in the press. It's a hard war to follow. It's a war in which there's no ammunition fired that didn't come from the Soviet Union or Communist China, because nothing is produced in the North. It all came through Hanoi or Phnom Penh or somewhere into South Vietnam; and the bulk of the fighting forces are now regular North Vietnamese. But still there was confusion about how much was invasion and how much civil war—a confusion which was played on with great cleverness in Communist propaganda. And yet I don't for a minute believe this country is ready to pull out of South Vietnam unilaterally.

HOWARD HANDLEMAN, *U.S. News & World Report*: Would either of you—we've had a lot of speculation both ways, one that the new administration is standing fast to the Vietnam policy of the Johnson Administration, and the other speculation is that there are great changes in the policy on Vietnam of the new administration.

Would each of you address yourself to that?

DR. GRIFFITH: Walt, do you want to begin?

MR. ROSTOW: I will not address myself to that.

(Laughter.)

DR. GRIFFITH: It seems to me that the funda-mental change in American policy in Vietnam with which we are dealing did not occur as a result of the change in administration but it occurred on March 31, 1968, when President Johnson announced the sus-pension of the bombing, his intention of going from that to negotiation, and his political abdication.

I think that the present administration has probably reinforced significantly this trend, but I don't think that they originated it. I think that the fundamental reason why he announced his political abdication was the change in American public opinion of which we have been speaking before.

(Laughter.)

MR. ROSTOW: I am familiar with this perspective. It has been widely published and President Johnson has commented upon it publicly. He said that it does not conform to the truth. I believe the documentary record will show that. This is not the occasion to lay out the story as it did happen. I would only repeat something, however, which I once said on television, so it's not new but it may give you a clue.

In talking to the Australian Cabinet in Canberra before Christmas 1967, President Johnson said that he thought the enemy was hungering for tactical victory.

He expected kamakazi tactics. It was for that reason that he had flown over the 101st Airborne and other units; but that when Hanoi came to the realization that its military efforts had failed the way might be opened to negotiation.

But there is in the public prints a number of analyses that could lead my distinguished colleague Professor Griffith to come to the judgment he expressed tonight. But it does not conform to the facts as I know them or as I believe the record will show them in time.

THOMAS W. WOLFE, RAND Corporation: There is a certain concern in many of the questions here about American staying power in one form or another.

I have an observation to make and I would invite your comment on it.

It seems to me that both our national experience with wars and our temperament tend to make us feel that wars, like other problems, run their own term and that you find solutions.

Now, it may very well be that the kind of role we are trying to play in the world is going to find us in situations where there just aren't solutions of this kind.

It seems to me the big question for us is can we learn to adapt ourselves to a role in the world where we may have to have long endurance and long staying power without finding the kinds of solutions to which we are temperamentally, sentimentally, and historically accustomed.

Do you think we have that kind of staying power?

DR. GRIFFITH: I think we have had it before. I think, however, that the experience with the Vietnam war to date shows that the calculations which must have been made by the political officials of this country, as to the tolerance of the American people for the period of time involved and the cost involved, were overoptimistic. And I think that because of this it will be much more difficult in the future, if anything similar to the Vietnam situation occurs, for us to deploy anything like the same amount of investment of men and money that has occurred in Vietnam.

I agree that this is the challenge.

I don't think the American public has turned out in the case of the Vietnam war to be willing to accept the challenge as they see it posed to them. And I fear this will make it much more difficult in the future for any similar challenge soon to be accepted again.

DR. LOWELL HARRISS, Columbia University: I think there is a saying it takes two to tango. We are talking about détente and a good deal has been said about public opinion in the United States.

Now, this is to either or both of you.

What do you know or can we judge about the development of public opinion in Russia and China with respect to the possibilities of détente?

(Laughter.)

MR. ROSTOW: I know very little about public opinion in the Soviet Union. And it is not a form of government that subjects itself systematically to the test of public opinion through the elective process.

And, therefore, I have based my own very measured long-term optimism—optimism only in the sense that I believe a movement towards peace is possible—not primarily on moods in and views within Soviet public opinion, but upon the changing shape of the world arena of power which by gradually denying certain options and even presenting certain dangers, may lead the Soviet Union to continue to take steps in the direction of détente and peace.

We have seen in parts of the world what parallelism looks like. We saw it during the Indo-Pak war. We hopefully are seeing a phase of some kind of parallelism in the Middle East, although how serious and effective that will be I do not know.

One can conceive of bases for parallelism in Southeast Asia, as well as South Asia.

And one can see reasons why the Soviet Union might wish to join with the United States in serious *measures* of arms control.

None of this has yet come to pass; but it is conceivable. But I would not base my argument that it might come to pass on public opinion in the Soviet Union. I would assume that the men, women, and children who live in the Soviet Union want peace as much or more than anyone.

I would assume that they are not tremendously excited about putting $300 million a year to keep Castro going or about various other expensive international enterprises that do not stem from public opinion.

As for Mainland China, as I tried to explain last time, Lowell, my view is that they are caught up in a very great debate indeed. Mao took a particular stance in the 1950s when he launched his first Five Year Plan. Like *Damn Yankee,* he never separated industrialization and modernization of the armed forces. He made six million cadre memorize chapters 9-12 of Stalin's short course history of the Bolshevik party of the Soviet Union, which were the chapters on the first Five Year Plan.

He behaved within his country as if China were where Russia was in 1931. In my judgment China was nearer where Japan was in the 1890s at the turn of the century. He neglected agriculture. He and his colleagues were tremendously anxious to generate the force to be a power on the world scene and in Asia. And that effort, Mao's underlying effort at modernization of China has not worked. They have had a ten-year period in which their statistics of production are very much like what they were in 1958 after going back and forth for a decade.

And a number of their enterprises on the world scene have not worked. I do believe that there are men who have come to the conclusion that their first job is to turn for some period of time to modernizing China. They look over at Taiwan, and they see it can be done.

If any nation, culturally or in terms of human material, has the capacity to build a modern nation, it is the Chinese.

And just as it has taken Castro great skill to neutralize $300 million a year in Soviet aid, it has taken Mao great skill to neutralize the natural capacity of the Chinese to modernize their nation—

(Laughter.)

—in terms of economic development. I think it will happen. But it won't be primarily because of public opinion; it will be because those who have some access to the instruments of power conclude that that is what China ought to do.

I would underline what I've said before: I have a kind of historical compassion for China's problems. They have had the hardest time of any nation in the world—after the intrusion of a more advanced West in the 1840s—in finding the formula to get on with the task of making a modern society. It has been more than a century—a century and a quarter almost of torment they have been through.

But it may be that in—I don't know what time period —three or five years, they will find some formula to bring it about.

Whatever their ambitions will then be—and I think the Chinese will still have large visions of their place in the world—they may *de facto* put their energies into modernizing their country. And for a time tactically, if you like, while still remembering the expansive maps that Mao has handed out to the schoolchildren—they will get on with the job at home.

But that is all you can hope for in the world. As China modernizes, however, Japan and the rest of Asia will continue to modernize and gain greater strength. In the arena of power that will emerge, with the Soviet Union on the one side and a modernized Asia on the other, in a generation or two the Chinese might look around and they might not then have extravagant dreams. The Chinese, in the end, are a practical people. Whatever else one says about the Chinese Communists, they have been, in fact, militarily cautious. They have undertaken no military adventure as dangerous, for example, as Khrushchev's putting missiles in Cuba.

PAUL NITZE, Johns Hopkins University: I would like to ask Mr. Griffith a question.

As I understood it, he said that he would put priority

upon our alliances with our major industrial allies.

If we do that, what happens with respect to that part of the world which isn't our major industrial ally?

DR. GRIFFITH: Well, I suppose that it will pursue the present course that I see it undertaking, which is not a very encouraging one.

I don't think, however, that what has been accomplished in terms of the constantly declining level of aid appropriations over the last few years indicates that no matter where we put our priorities, the people of this country will unfortunately not put up the kind of money for aid appropriations which would be required to make a major change in this respect.

We have been prepared to do this with respect to the imminent threat of hunger in the case of India, although of course it has been very convenient for our wheat surplus for a while.

We have been prepared to do it in those rare instances where we are convinced that our strategic interests are involved.

But I wasn't really trying to contrast priority for our developed allies with the priority for the Third World, because I don't think in fact we ever have given priority to the Third World and I don't think we will.

I was trying to contrast it with respect to priority to Western Europe and Japan as opposed to priority to negotiation with the Soviet Union.

It seems to me that in this instance we would be well advised to give priority to our allies, notably Western Europe and Japan, for a series of reasons, not the least of which is that it seems to me that this is probably the most effective way for us to deal with the Soviet Union and China.

MARTIN CLANCY, Senate Republican Policy Committee: Professor Rostow, do I understand you correctly to say that—I just wanted to clarify this—a USSR-U.S. détente could work to the advantage or be welcomed by Hanoi as a base for aid and so on as against the Chinese threat?

MR. ROSTOW: I was being highly speculative. What I said was that in my judgment, for what it's worth, the long-run security problem of the people who live around Hanoi is their independence of China. It has been so for a long time. It is likely to remain so. Therefore, the notion that the United States and the Soviet Union may find in Southeast Asia a certain parallelism of interest might command itself to Hanoi at a time of peace. It might give them a bit of breathing room to make their dispositions as an independent nation. I find it significant that they are sending their emissaries to discuss postwar reconstruction in places where you would not normally suspect they would go, as if they were trying to build up a set of connections which would give them some breathing room as an independent nation.

But a great deal depends on whether they can fulfill their dream in South Vietnam and Laos. Ho is not a young man. He and his colleagues have dreamed all their mature lives of succeeding to the French Colonial Empire in Asia. They've violated international understandings that they undertook as late as 1962, with a sense of private legitimacy. This was their dream.

But if that dream's not going to come off, they're going to have to make a nation that lives up there and develops itself as best it can. Knowing the Vietnamese I think that they can do quite a lot, even though they will be borne down by collectivization in agriculture. I think the South Vietnamese are going to come ahead faster than the South Koreans after the war.

If the North Vietnamese are going to find their future in a narrower terrain than their dream of glory—in, for example, a long-run peaceful relation to South Vietnam and the rest of Southeast Asia—I think that they might want to see U.S.-Soviet détente develop in Southeast Asia for very narrow security reasons.

MR. CLANCY: You are saying détente would increase the hostility between China and the USSR?

MR. ROSTOW: That's a much more complex matter which doesn't hinge so much on Southeast Asia but on the total relationship between Russia and China. It's a big, separate subject. I don't want to get into it, unless that's what you all want to do.

AMBASSADOR LOY W. HENDERSON: I'd like to ask both of our speakers if in their opinion the United States government could come to a détente with countries like China and the Soviet Union under conditions which would guarantee our own national security, unless it has the support of the people of our own country, including our intellectual leaders?

It seems to me that for a number of years our universities have been tending to glorify dissent and to look with contempt on those who are inclined to rally behind the foreign and internal policies of our government.

I have observed in past years similar tendencies to glorify dissent in a number of other countries which were experimenting in democracy and in practically every instance democracy has proved a failure.

DR. GRIFFITH: I agree with Ambassador Henderson that we will only be able to carry on an effective détente with the Soviet Union or China or both if we have adequate support for it in this country, including among intellectual leaders in universities and elsewhere.

I would add only that I think that the dissent in universities among intellectuals with U.S. government policy has not been primarily with respect to détente. It has been rather, if anything, that the dissenters feel that the U.S. government has not given enough priority to détente.

So that I would not think in this particular case that the problem would be with what you call the intellectual leaders of the country.

AMBASSADOR HENDERSON: I'm referring to dissent in general.

DR. GRIFFITH: More generally I think that this is perfectly true as of the present time as compared to, say, five years ago or ten years ago, but I am old enough to remember back to the late 1930s, when dissent among intellectuals and students with policies of the U.S. government was at least as great, if not greater.

I remember a statement by some 400 leading intellectuals just the week before the Soviet-Nazi pact, including, oh, people like Mary McCarthy and so on—(I think Susan Sontag was not old enough to sign it then.) (Laughter.)—declaring that the imperious calumny that the Soviet Union could ever sign a pact with the Nazis was a particularly vicious slander. Moscow did sign a week thereafter, with the reverberations of which you are aware.

I must also add that in the 1930s there were several major trade unions in this country under effective Communist control. This is no longer the case.

I think that the most alarming cause of the dissent probably is the Vietnam war. If that could be concluded, it would help to lower it. But I think that the much greater, longer-term causes relate to the problems of poverty and the treatment of the blacks, and the concern, as Walt has pointed out, with the dehumanization aspects of a technocratic society.

These I think could easily be handled, as he has said. The growth every year in our GNP makes this quite easy. The problem unfortunately is, it seems to me, that for the near future the majority of the white middleclass and much of the workingclass of this country simply isn't prepared to put up the money.

ARNOLD KOTZ, Stanford Research Institute: My question is for Dr. Rostow.

Professor Griffith mentioned that he thought a major thrust in Vietnam should be in the political and social development areas and, if negotiations at some time in the future are successful, the central foci will then be on these two areas.

To what extent are the developments with the South Vietnamese competitive now in social progress with the Communists and what are the specifics of the social projects you indicated as taking place today in Vietnam?

MR. ROSTOW: There's a war going on in the South. It is, of course, disruptive. But looking at the prospects, all the prospects are more favorable in the South, with one exception I'll take up at the end.

First of all, both countries are primarily agricultural.

You already have quite a substantial quiet agricultural revolution going on in South Vietnam. They are absorbing the IR-8 rice seeds more rapidly than almost any other country in the world. They've got a chicken revolution going, a cheap protein revolution, and they have the Mekong.

The farmers in areas with regular access to the cities —and these are quite substantial—are already moving forward. You can already see the signs of the dynamics of the market. They've got small pumps. They've got chemical fertilizers. They have the seeds. They are beginning to move beyond the bicycle to the Labretta and the sewing machine. The modernization of rural life has palpably begun in certain areas. It could go very fast economically in peace.

Second, you've had the beginnings in Saigon of an industrial revolution in small shops undertaking metal fabrication and plastic fabrication as well as some modern textile industry. Some plant was damaged in Tet; but, I gather, it's coming back.

Third, and most impressive, I think you've got David Lilienthal's inspiration. I put it that way because he's been extremely careful to make postwar planning a Vietnamese not an American operation. An able young group is now planning economic reconstruction and development. It is doing the job not in aggregative terms; that is by calculations of investment rates, a capital-out-put ratio and GNP increased—but doing it practically, region by region.

On the economic side I have no doubt that with the vital agricultural sector, which they have naturally, not being collectivized, and on the basis of a light industry base and the resources of the country—and with the kind of help they could get from abroad and absorb quickly, the South Vietnamese could go ahead at least as fast as South Korea has gone in this decade.

Socially, they have some land reform problems to solve. There are some rather intelligent plans formulated. But it is not a country where the land reform problem is central, because it is not a place of truly big estates. The central land reform question really concerns the absentee landlord: whether you can convert some of his tenants into owners; and giving firm title to people who have been holding land—and farming it —where the landowners have left. There has been some good staff work done. A lot of land has been redistributed; but we all know that land reform work is hard work. It's an important issue but manageable. I think there is a political and staff-work basis for intelligent land reform policies in South Vietnam.

The biggest question mark for South Vietnam versus the North is the one with which they are now wrestling. It is, as I said earlier, the endemic question for developing democracies: whether they can build, out of a prior

history of fractional fragmentation, the habits of mutual consultation and compromise which would permit
them a big national but not monopolistic political party,
or coalition.

That is what Thieu is now working towards. It's the
lesson that the Vietnamese have drawn from examining
their own problems, their own weaknesses as well as the
experiences of other developing nations in constitutional
democracy.

The asset which you have in a developing nation to
compensate for the great human burdens of a single-
party dictatorship—the asset you've got is political stability. The real challenge the South Vietnamese face is
to build the institutions that would permit them, if you
like, to run one or two candidates, not 11, against a
Communist front in free elections; and then to go on
from that to build a national party which will provide
a stable base for governmental policies of development.

I know the history of South Vietnam tolerably well.
I think that there are a few areas where their own history combined with the colonial experience make the
prospects for this less *prima facie* promising. But because of that they have worked at it harder than almost
anyone else. They know this is their problem. They cannot live successfully as an independent nation under 11
candidates for the presidency.

So, in the figure of speech I quoted last week in another context, the sight of the gallows has tended to concentrate their minds rather wonderfully in moving them towards the building of a political base that might win in the election and give them some stability.

That is the biggest task, because the rest of the job is clearly possible. It's not a hungry country. It's got good land. It's got able people. It's got a peasantry that's voracious in the absorption of education; and with some seeds and fertilizers and pumps, those farmers know just what crops to choose, when to get into the market and when to get out. They do arithmetic awfully well.

And with that kind of an agricultural base and some industrialization and light industry, a modernized fishing industry, tourism—they'll do all right.

FOOTNOTES

SECOND LECTURE

[1] Quoted from *Studies on Viet Nam*, Department of External Affairs, Canberra, Australia, August 1965, p. 23. Minister of Defense Giap made the statement on the tenth anniversary of the Geneva Agreement of 1954 (July 19, 1964, in *Nhan Dan*).

[2] For the author's view of this complex relationship, see *The Dynamics of Soviet Society*, Second edition (New York: W. W. Norton & Company, 1967), pp. 6-11.

[3] See for example, the author's *The Stages of Economic Growth* (Cambridge: Cambridge University Press, 1960), pp. 102-03.

REBUTTALS

Walt W. Rostow

[1] I shall not go into certain minor differences of emphasis; for example, the question of whether the cold war was inevitable. As I argued in *The United States in the World Arena* (New York: Harper & Row, 1960), I happen to believe it was not inevitable. For example the role of United States trade as an instrument of influence: I would not rate our external influence as spreading "primarily through economic expansion." For example, the nature of our concern with Castro: The danger he poses is not merely Cuba as a Russian base but also the pressures he exerts as a base for the sending of men, arms, and money across international frontiers for purposes of terrorism and guerrilla warfare in the rest of Latin America.

$5.75

WILLIAM E. GRIFFITH, Professor of Political Science at the Massachusetts Institute of Technology and Professor of Soviet Diplomacy at the Fletcher School of Law and Diplomacy, Tufts University, is the author of a two-volume work on *Communism in Europe*, published by M.I.T. Press. Three other works dealt with the developing split between Communist China and the Soviet Union: *Sino-Soviet Relations, 1964-65*; *The Sino-Soviet Rift*; and *Albania and The Sino-Soviet Rift*, all published by M.I.T. Press. From 1951 to 1958 he was political adviser to Radio Free Europe in Munich.

WALT WHITMAN ROSTOW, Professor of Economics and History, University of Texas, has been an adviser to Presidents since the Eisenhower years. A graduate of Yale University and a Rhodes Scholar, he was perhaps best known as President Johnson's Special Assistant for National Security Affairs from 1966 to 1969; earlier he served in the Kennedy and Johnson Administrations as chairman of the State Department's Policy Planning Council. His major publications include: *The Stages of Economic Growth, A Non-Communist Manifesto*; *The United States in the World Arena*; *The Dynamics of Soviet Society*; *The Prospects for Communist China* and *View From the Seventh Floor*.